Lecture Notes in Educational Technology

Series editors

Ronghuai Huang
Kinshuk
Mohamed Jemni
Nian-Shing Chen
J. Michael Spector

Lecture Notes in Educational Technology

The series *Lecture Notes in Educational Technology* (LNET), has established itself as a medium for the publication of new developments in the research and practice of educational policy, pedagogy, learning science, learning environment, learning resources etc. in information and knowledge age, – quickly, informally, and at a high level.

More information about this series at http://www.springer.com/series/11777

Elena Aurel Railean

User Interface Design of Digital Textbooks

How Screens Affect Learning

 Springer

Elena Aurel Railean
Institute for Advanced Study at Moscow
    State Pedagogical University
Moscow
Russia

and

European University of Moldova
Chişinău
Moldova

and

Tiraspol State University
Chişinău
Moldova

ISSN 2196-4963   ISSN 2196-4971   (electronic)
Lecture Notes in Educational Technology
ISBN 978-981-10-2455-9   ISBN 978-981-10-2456-6   (eBook)
DOI 10.1007/978-981-10-2456-6

Library of Congress Control Number: 2016948807

Printed on acid-free paper

This Springer imprint is published by Springer Nature
The registered company is Springer Nature Singapore Pte Ltd.
The registered company address is: 152 Beach Road, #22-06/08 Gateway East, Singapore 189721, Singapore

This book is dedicated to my children and my parents that provides advances, life tools and values necessary to be their where I am today. The inspiration for doing the research in frontier area of pedagogy come from the post-doctoral program aims to investigate correlations between digital learning theory and design. This post-doctoral program was one of the most important and formative in my life, enabling to do research in various countries.

My thanks and appreciation to all Professors and specialists in pedagogy, psychology, knowledge management, informatics, instructional and learning design from USA, Romania, Russian Federation, Germany, Switzerland, Finland, Greece, Republic of Moldova, Turkey and Canada who shared their meticulous research experiences, methodologies and insights that supported and expanded my own work in pedagogy of the digital textbook use and development.

I must acknowledge also colleagues, friends, teachers, and students from different universities and schools around the world who listed, assisted, advised, and supported my writing efforts over this three years long project. Especially, I need to express my gratitude and deep appreciation to Professor George Rudic, Centre of Modern Pedagogy whose understanding of the philosophy of globalisation, postmodernism, and education challenges on learning has enlightened me to keep motivation in research for many years.

Preface

What interface design of digital textbooks do we need for twenty-first century students? Should printed textbooks digitized or digitalized? How important is to identify issues before the design of affordable digital textbooks? How should digital textbooks be designed and developed? Who and why should develop digital textbooks? In order to understand how to respond to these questions it is important to accept that metasystems learning design of digital textbooks is a trend for sustainable education and innovative decision-making processes, activities, and actions. These questions inspired the ideas presented in this book.

The initiative to replace printed textbooks with digital textbooks provides unrivalled functional content that allow discovering new ways of learning, but also inhibit learning. Nevertheless, most of the learning designers and educational policy makers believe that digital textbooks are only the digitalised version of the printed textbooks and they do not want to think about the learner and learning. This causes a misunderstanding of the pedagogy as a frontier science and leads on many projects without any impact on successful learning.

But digital textbooks theory and practice is a hot area of frontier research between pedagogy, psychology, philosophy, cybernetics, and knowledge management. User interface design is the main topic in this area. The research question of the proposed author book: *How screens affect learning*? is focused on investigation the correlations between learning theory and practice in using and development of digital textbooks in order to synthesis the main theoretical questions for applied research.

What the proposed research question is so important? First, because data, information and knowledge on digital screens mainly appears as abstract information and not as a (meta)cognitive tool for sense-making, decision, and communication. Thus, in many cases digital textbooks are designed for reading and not for development of the practical skills. Second, the most acclaimed feature of the digital textbooks is in *affordability*. This issue is common for digital reading because it takes longer time and requires more efforts to reach the same level of understanding than on printed version, even in a controlled digital learning environment. It was observed, for example, that transferring the printed page of textbooks into PDF is a more convenient access to distractions than for learning. The scanning pattern from reading on digital screens is less intensive and takes longer time than when the student reads a printed paragraph. These and many other facts allow to establish the importance of research in user interface design of digital textbooks in accordance with the real problems of learning and not only with a digital fashion.

Students prefer digital textbooks for its lower price they are less heavy instead of printed textbooks. But, digital content may embody, also, the immediate feedback, animation, simulations, networking, extension of provided content and other interactive features. In the same way, digital reading on screen is harder when designers ignore norms, provided by paradigm. Maybe, design science should find a new way to make digital screen affordable for learning.

According to scientific research, opinions of students regarding the efficiency of the digital textbooks are contradictory. Thus, the survey taken in USA shows that 57.8 % of students prefer digital textbooks over the printed versions. The other survey, reported by Schaub (2016) provides the evidence that 92 % of college students prefer print books instead of e-books because printed textbooks are less distractive. Therefore, user interfaces of digital textbooks require an ecological way that allow a new understanding of educational technology.

Changing the way in which digital textbooks interfaces will be designed is a FRONTIER PEDAGOGY theme, especially because it is applied MetaSystems Learning Design principles for solving real issues in a practical way. *The aim of the book is to synthesize correlations between theory and practice, especially those related of changing paradigms.* Subject line relies on digital textbooks effectiveness for sustainable education, as an attempt to validate the MetaSystems Learning Design principles for guaranteed learning outcomes.

User interface design of digital textbooks are presented from the perspectives of the linear, systems, and holistic (metasystems) approaches. The readers will gain understanding of the terminology, overall user interface design phases, the design of specific mechanisms, processes, and pedagogical scenarios. It provides guidelines regarding how to identify and design learning objects, how to develop pedagogical scenarios, how to embody students in instructional design process and how to develop an open digital textbook.

The central focus of the author book is on how digital screens affect learning. Five chapters of the book discuss the following: impacts of digital revolution on learning; a paradigm shift and user interface design models; digital screens and issues of multiliteracies learning; teacher-centered versus learner-centered design of screen; knowledge ecology and sustainable development. The book was written to provide a single reference point for all interested in user interface design. Beginners and the experienced users of digital textbooks alike will find information they need to cover nearly transdisciplinary theories, models of learning, principles, and norms required to use and to develop digital textbooks in and for a sustainable education.

Chişinău, Moldova   Elena Aurel Railean
2016

Contents

Chapter 1
Impacts of Digital Revolution on Learning

Design is the action of bringing something new and desired into existence—a proactive stance that resolves or dissolves problematic situations by design. It is a compound of routine, adaptive and design expertise brought to bear on complex dynamic situations.

Harold Nelson

Abstract Digital revolution changes mechanical to digital technologies and establishes new requirements for instruction, assessment and learning mechanisms and processes, which can be defined under the umbrella of education 3.0 on challenges coming from the expected new industrial revolution. Although education system become more open and flexible, there are many confusion issues during the interface design process. One of this is size, diversity and availability of digital screens. How screens affect learning and, therefore, the interface design process of the digital textbooks? This scientific question inspired the ideas presented in this chapter. The chapter describes the specific features of the digital revolution' phases and their impacts on literacy, competence development and didactic triangle.

Keywords Digital revolution · Literacy · Didaktik triangle

1.1 Introduction

Since the late of 1950 until the late of 1970s in many places of the world has started the Digital Revolution. This revolution changes the mechanical and electronic technology to digital technology and cyber physical systems and starts the complex renovation of schools, adding computers in special classrooms. Now, adoption and proliferation of digital computers to schools are everywhere in the world. Many projects aims to develop and to use digital textbooks. These cause a deep interest in digital textbooks. However, some projects are not successful as was expected according to project proposal. What are the reasons?

E.A. Railean, *User Interface Design of Digital Textbooks*,
Lecture Notes in Educational Technology, DOI 10.1007/978-981-10-2456-6_1

Digital revolution is one of the greatest revolution, which changes not only the technology, but also the model of human thinking of how to design learning environments and learning. In this context, new communication patterns have developed for formal, informal and non-formal education. Digital or/and digitized textbooks are developed and disseminated globally. In addition, digital screens are everywhere, including our hands and unexpected places. However; user interface design of widely disseminated screens is more universal and less adapted to users' needs, even if it is focusing on user. What are the users' needs: to learn something new, to be informed about some news or/and to develop the competence? Does these screens affect learning with traditional printed textbooks? If yes, in which way?

Digital revolution affects education and, therefore, learning. This issue could be investigated using 'ideal type' methodology of the qualitative research. In our case was studied the 'custom level' of theory and practice, allowing us to identify three phases of the digital revolution impacts for education 1.0, education 2.0 and education 3.0, respectively.

At the level of education 1.0 the theory was investigated instructional design of programmed textbooks and automatized systems, but the practice—development of the digitised versions of printed textbooks and educational software. Moreover, theory and practice of the programmed textbooks and educational software within East and West countries was based on two different models: problem-solving and tutorial-learning.

The problem is that in a very short time, static education of 1.0 was changed rapidly through interactivity, adaptive and flexible systems with Artificial Intelligence mechanism and social media (education 2.0) with the shared educational economy and networking (education 3.0). An inevitable way was changing the user-interface design principles of digital textbooks from universal design through instructional systems design to metasystems learning design. The MetaSystems Learning Design argues that 'meta X' is more than a sum of X in terms of organisation, logics and analysing of data. Why instructional system design is so applicable?

To understand the essence of the metasystems learning design approach it is important to identify the state-of-art in all areas that are or/and may be connected to solve a practical issue. In our case this issue is: How screens affect learning?, which is transformed into the research question. To best way to identify the state-of-art in is the historical method. First, accounts have identified through synthesis of data provided by the primary sources of philosophy, psychology, learning theory and instructional design and its correlation with digital revolution phases. This allow to identify cross-principles and new functions of digital textbooks.

Second, only digital revolution discovers new and 'an emerging field of study, combining the philosophy of technology and information theory, with critical pedagogy and educational philosophy' (Lewin and Lundie 2016). The French philosopher of contemporary technology, Stiegler (2016, p. 157) notes that digital marks an immense transformations, those impact explodes all frames of thinking. Computerisation is very different from digitalisation. Therefore, the emergence of digitalisation printed textbooks in comparison with the computerisation and networking of society is only one factor of the global challenges that affect learning. While most teachers and practitioners designers look at the learning process roughly the same as their colleagues did in XVI–XIX century; informational, communicational and learning environments outside them 'has been exploding every day' taking away students from reading pictorial textbooks in order to place them in a digital environment.

Our students today have, at least one digital device. The philosophes have traced a connection between of the transformative power of technology in education and digital literacy development among young people. Plowman (2016, pp. 96–103) has argued that learning technology is not a term associated with the early years of childhood. In addition, in the field of research on technology-enhanced learning the emphases is more often of the technology than on learning. However, some of the special features of textbooks on e-readers or touchscreen tablets could motivate children to read include animation, read about narration, an easier accessible dictionary with spoken pronunciation, and the faculty to highlight, annotate and enlarge text, although both books and e-reading devices can be sharable, mobile and portable.

Can the designed screen so that to affect didactic process? From one hand, the promise that digital screen will revolutionise teaching, assessment and learning through, for example, the interactive or open content, passed away without any comments. From the other hand, the multimodal texts with image, music, and speech are everywhere. Frequent, but short length multimodal text that can be messaging/associated everywhere and anytime. This is a more cost-effective and time-consuming than developing of traditional textbooks. If so, what principles and norms are? According to metasystems approach, digital screen for learning should be designed according to state-of-art in design and all domains that investigate the issue, expected to be solved at the level of design and its practical application.

One more question, which is related to sustainable development of the world. All peoples are different in terms of openness, communication, mobility, IQ and so on. However, Kaplan (2015, p. 2) has argued that the "hereditarian" hypothesis with respect to differences in average IQ between population is not supported with empirical research. How could be these differences 'be included' in user interface design of digital textbooks? Are this an example of adaptive education? If yes, how these principles correlate with sustainable education?

Rejecting the traditional pedagogy models on reading instructional objectives and delivering the content via voice, text or video, contemporary pedagogy contends their adepts that is better to learn metacognitive strategies and to apply them in solving real problems than read or view video about their importance. However, metacognitive strategies is a complex issue. Being a part of sustainable education in learning with/without digital textbooks metacognitive strategies are part of the solution in contemporary education.

This chapter reflects on user interface design of digital textbooks for sustainable education through correlation of issues and solutions regarding how digital screen impacts learning. It examines digital revolution phases in accordance with educational technologies. The range of topics to cover the proposed subject of the book is nearly limited, so of course it has been impossible to include everything there is to say on all examined concepts. Therefore, it was tried the cover the most important and common ones.

1.2 Challenges of the Digital Revolution on Learning

Digital revolution has passed three significant phases:

– data processing technologies and personal computing (1950–1971)
– multimedia, Social Media and network computing (1982–1990)
– cloud computing and global connection with Internet (2007–2011).

1.2.1 Data Processing Technologies and Personal Computing for Extrinsic Motivation Issues

Data processing technologies and personal computers changes the world of education and methods of learning in 1950. In the 1960s, J. Bruner helped spearhead a revolution in psychology, emphasizing learning through interpersonal interactions and exploring such topics as how we gain meaning through those interactions as well as how the mind deals with the information it is given. In the same years were proposed various Cognitive Taxonomies, instructional design models, teaching machines, computer-based assessment.

However, these ideas were developed only by technical (e.g. informational and communicational technologies, automatized systems of instruction and others) implementation in educational technology. There are some examples: the first computer-assisted learning system 'PLATO' (1960) and the first adoption of microcomputers in public education (1970). Moreover, if the pedagogy proposed the idea of personalised learning (F. Keller), the technology developed only the experimental model of individual learning in a computer environment.

Theory slowly moves from behavioural to cognitive science. It was written many interesting books: 'The Science of Learning and the Art of Teaching' (Skinner 1954), Taxonomy of Educational Objectives (Bloom 1956), System of instruction (Glaser 1962); and The conditions of learning (Gagne 1985) and others. As was noted by Coulson and Cogswell (1965, p. 59): 'in programed instruction the learning pace is set by the individual student; moreover, if the program provides 'branching' capabilities, the sequence also is individualised'. All these innovations are based on immediate feedback and systems approach. Thus, development of systems for instruction and the individual testing procedures could be considered the main impact of the first phase of the digital revolution on learning.

How screen had been affected learning in the first phase of the digital revolution? A type recorder or motion picture can act as a standard instruction stimulus. The practical solution was motion pictures. Zinn (1967, p. 618) notes that typically the users converse with the computers through direct connections of electric type-writers, film projectors, audio devices, electronic display screens, and pointers. Therefore, at the earliest stage of revolution using projectors for pictures or/and motion pictures has been the centrepiece to integrate technology into classroom, helping students to be extremely motivated to learn with motion pictures.

It was expected that the digital screen would attract and maintain the students' attention, increasing motivation and contributing to knowledge. There are contra-dictive data regarding how learning outcomes correlate with patterns. What is true, screens allow using impressive features, such as zoom and high-definition imagery of pictures allowing data to be stored and transmitted, for teaching/learning music and foreign languages.

Nonetheless, while digital devices have been embedded in school life, the learning theory are struggling to keep up instruction within of the Comenius tra-dition. This fact cause misunderstandings of results can be obtained, while learning with technology is in the adequate way for guaranteed outcomes. Comenius wrote about the importance of mathetics as a solution for learning: *Mathetics is not didactics, but a science about how to learn in the most effective way*. This fact could be considered the first attempt to theoretically separate instruction from learning. This indicated to the first discrepancy between design models, systems and tools for learning and mathetics, as a theory of learning issues and its practical solutions.

Starting the rapid challenges of the electronic display screens it is another of the big challenges of the first digital revolution on learning. Thus, a key advance in electronic display screens comes from rapid changes in cathode ray tube from monochrome to direct-view bistable storage tube, flip-disk display, monochrome plasma display, light-emitting diode, vacuum fluorescent display, twisted nematic effects LCD and pin screen. All of these innovations in formal schooling were used, but the most important thing is everybody could buy personal computers. Peoples were interested to learn in a computer environment because it was more motivated. The provided simulations, animations and feedback capture attention. This means that at the end of the first phase of the digital revolution, the learning become as formal as informal.

One more invention has challenged the world of education: Nicholas K. Sheridon from Xerox PARC, of the Gyricon proposed the first model of the electronic paper. With the specific feature of monochrome, the electronic paper 'opens' the door for new learning patterns and objects which changed the traditional methods of reading, writing and studying chemistry, physics, biology, mathematics and foreign languages. However, the electronic paper together with information-communication technologies open one more way, known as *adapta-tion*. There are many examples, e.g. MINERVA—an adaptive computing system with learning networks, which provides feedback to switch network regarding the information gaited on a different set of terminals (Aleksander 1975). The second example is zero adaptation, because user interface design was minimalized to digitized patterns of books and archive cultural works, but the most important here is the *open format of digitised books*, which discover the way of open access.

1.2.2 Multimedia, Social Media and Network Computing

Multimedia and network computing defines the second phase of digital revolution. Staring from the 1975 a personal relatively inexpensive computer could be buy for the individual use. Immediately the primary focus on personal computers was *intuitive learning*. Thus, first computers have already used the *graphical user interface* with windows, icons, and a mouse. Moreover, they had the specific features that allows connections via local networks, sharing files and printing out documents. At the end of the second phase, the graphical user interface, proposed by Microsoft Windows and the Apple Macintosh, was widely accepted.

Projectors' technology moved to a *data projector model*, which allows taking signals from a computer or television, and projects an image on a projection screen. Through the main results of this phase can be identified the oral communication of teacher's speech which has been reinforced by technology. Therefore, students not only can read, write and recall information from memory, but also received a new tool helping to understand phenomenon, mechanisms, processes and abstract things in a deepest way.

Nevertheless, by the end of twenty century, written computer-assisted testing were developed in all countries, especially for vocational education. If we believed data of empirical research, the oral communication in testing has been on a downward spiral in favour of writing examination. Moreover, research thematic moves from programed instruction to learning algorithms and multimedia education in all others, based on behaviourism and cognitivism. In addition, were developed: psychological properties of digital learning nets (Aleksander 1970); pattern recognition using random-access memories (Aleksander and Stonham 1979), developing of instructional objectives and multimedia cognitive load theory and many others.

It is not surprised for us that most of the research is focused on understanding digital learning nets and on processing the complex multimedia information at the level of human brain. First, digital learning nets relies on pattern recognition as 'a relationship between the data and the defined classification categories' (Stonham and Shaw 1975). Second, in analysing digital learning nets was used new terms: visual perception, system, artificial intelligence, stochastic processes, dynamic programing, pattern recognition, feedback, and reinforcement learning.

However, theoretically computers in education relies on reinforcement learning. But, the reinforcement learning is the area of the investigation the learning algorithms. The learning algorithms is not only the cause-effect. Although specialists in experimental psychology have extended Skinner's theory, disputing the presumed significant advantage of only the computer environment for learning (Lubow et al.

1976; Elio and Anderson 1984); some variables on the computer screens remains commonplace, e.g. density of displayed text, scrolling, upper-case versus upper- and lower-case lettering, letter size, and graphics. According to Hathaway (1984), the specific variables on the screen mostly affect learning.

Does these variables provide an informational or/and emotional load at the students' learning capacity? Developments in the experimental psychology at that time demonstrated 'how affect may bias the processing of self-relevant information and help to clarify the links between affect and person variables in the cognitive social learning framework' (Wright and Mischel 1982). This vision was for everyone on the globe to be with the limited capacity of proceeding the complex information on screen and to work at computer. However, for the first time researchers have begun to acknowledge the importance of the emotional variables at the design level, although the practical application of these finding to learning design remains nascent.

The second phase of the digital revolution materialised when the importance of the *self-directed learning* issues were highlighted. Knowles (1975) defined self-directed learning within teacher-directed learning, showing that human being grows in capacity (and need) to be self-directed as an essential component of maturing self-directed learning and that this capacity should be nurtured in order to be developed as rapidly as possible. The idea of using the learners' experiences as an increasingly rich resource for learning is the most interesting. But, what this means in reality: knowledge about own knowledge, processing information presented on screen or the energy to get the presented information? According to Knowles (1975, p. 18):

> in its broadest meaning, 'self-directed learning' describes a process by which individuals take the initiative, with our without the assistance of others, in diagnosing their learning needs, formulating learning goals, identify human and material resources for learning, choosing and implement appropriate learning strategies, and evaluating learning outcomes.

The ideas to connect computers in a local networking for reinforcement and self-directed learning are the main premise in development of the *Social Learning Theory* (Bandura 1977, p. 2). According to this theory, the humans' capacity of learning by observation enables them to acquire large, integrated units of behaviour by example, without having to build up the patterns gradually through trial and errors. The superior cognitive capacity determines the future actions. Moreover, the human is capable of creating self-regulative influences by effective managing the stimulus. Instead of reinforcement theories, assuming that imitative responses must be reinforced in order to be learning, social learning theory distinguishing between learning and performances (Fig. 1.1).

Anticipated S ^{reinf} $\Longrightarrow$ Attention $\Longrightarrow$ S$_{modeling}$ $\Longrightarrow$ Symbolic coding/Cognitive organisation/Rehearsal $\Longrightarrow$ R

Fig. 1.1 Social learning theory (According to Bandura 1977, p. 9)

In Social Learning Theory, reinforcement is facultative rather than a necessary condition. Hence, when children intently watching modelled actions on a television screen in a darkened room displayed the same amount of imitative learning regardless of what they were previously informed. Behaviour is regulated both by directly experienced consequences from external sources and by vicarious reinforcement and self-reinforcement. The major function of modelling stimuli is to transmit information into *new patterns of behaviour*, which can be conveyed through physical demonstration, pictorial representation or verbal description.

But, what means the new patterns of behaviour? According to Social Learning Theory, the human functioning relies on three regulatory processes, which are *stimulus control, cognitive control* and *reinforcement control*. The stimulus control relies on human's capacity to gain information from the environmental stimulus in order to anticipate and to regulate his/her behaviour according to the probable consequences of various events and courses of action. The cognitive control is about the thinking modelling. With the framework of Social Learning Theory, the reinforcement is not either responsible for learning.

There are many external influences like television, films and pictorial displays. All external informational-communicational sources affect learning, enabling children and adults to acquire new attitudes, emotional responses and a copy-behaviour, based on new behavioural patterns. Indeed, new patterns of behaviour may results because of *perceptual learning*. From the psychological point of view, 'the controlled search is highly demanding of attentional capacity serial in nature with a limited comparison rate, is easily established, altered and even reversal by the subject, and is strongly dependent of load. Automatic detection is relatively well learned in long-term memory, is demanding of attention only when a target is presented, is parallel in nature, is difficult to alter, to ignore, or to suppress once learned, and is virtually unaffected by load' (Shiffrin and Schneider 1977, p. 127). A recent application of the Social Learning Theory to may be considered *Social Adaptive Interfacing*, which is 'a multi-dimensional interface for repository collections which brings forward information pertaining to previous navigation trials from various starting points on the users current location' (Coyle et al. 2016).

In addition, multimedia and network computing re-focused research in psychology from behavioural to cognitive science. It was developed multimedia applications, as well as interrelated tools and applications, multimedia information system, multimedia conferencing systems and others. Many of multimedia elemenents were important to *multimedia textbooks*, a type of digital textbook, when content is presented to learners visually or an equivalent to educational software that present the content for learning through multimodal text, e.g. as a combination of text, hypertext, sound, pictures, graphics, videos and animations. All systems and theirs interfaces could be analysed on the base on SAMR Model (where S—Substitution; A—Augmentation; M—Modification and R—Redefinition), developed by Dr. Ruben Puentedura (Table 1.1).

Of course, even that multimedia textbooks widely adoption for school learning, acknowledge that there may be problems with the positive impact of certain specific techniques for deeper learning. Here it is an assumed fact, which proved that during

Table 1.1 Digitized learning versus digital learning

SAMR	Digitized learning	Digital learning
	S, A	M, R
Assessment	Students read from an online textbook rather than write answers to the chapter Questions on paper	Students are engaged in interactive assessment or they are asked to reflect on the provided information, to develop an opinion or to create a product that defence their opinions based on evidence
Learning	No creativity or critical thinking	To design and to share an authentic project for feedback, even global

learning with digitized textbooks there is no evidence concerning affordance of digital reading in principle, but only in specific contexts. Maybe, from these reasons were developed the Dale' Cone of Learning. This, according to Dale, after two weeks the students will remember only 10 % from what read, 20 % of what was listened, 30 % of what viewed, 50 % of what was listened and viewed, 70 % of what said and 90 % of what said and done (Howard 2013; Greenfield 2013; Morrarty 2013).

1.2.3 Internet, Evolution of the Web for 1.0, 2.0 and 3.0 Education

There is, also, an intermediary period, known as global networking, when the Earth has linked with computers in order to share data or resources, even educational. First, society receives the possibility to widely use the web in various aims. Digitalisation is adopted technology of converting text, sound, photos, and video into data that can be processes by digital devices. Second, digitalisation opens the question regarding the future of the digitised textbooks and open education or/and to disseminate information regarding developed CD/DVD. However, to do this is important to have clear and intuitive interfaces.

There are many innovations in user interface design, which definitely change the world of education. Three of them: digital light processing, full-color plasma display and reinvention of the electronic paper have marked the evolution of web and graphical design. Over the next two decades, a great progress in user interfaces design has observed. First, it was coined new terms, like user interface design progress, interface designers, user experience design, prototyping, engaging and usable interfaces, visual hierarchy, navigational distance, user interface patterns, the use of colors, multi-touch screen, multi-use content, mobile interfaces and others. Second, it was developed many practical applications of these terms and it was developed some design principles, based on textual-communicational, mobile and gestural interactions.

Internet, website and multimedia systems were widely adopted. They allows, at least, developing a special type of digital textbooks, known as *interactive textbooks* (Fisher and Koryllos 1998) or *online interactive textbooks* (Smith 2000; Schwarz et al. 2005). The interactive textbooks were beyond conventional printed textbooks in delivering information and in active engagement of all students in the learning process. However, as was noted by Smith (2000), textbooks reflect the bias and approach of the author(s), and limit in some matter every instructor who adopts it to the particular approach and organisation of the didactic material. That is why digital textbooks are used as supplements to lectures and often the relationships between what the students read and hear in class is not clear.

On the web 1.0 the digital textbooks represents, mainly, the *static hypertext* (Brusilovsky et al. 2003), which immediately opens many questions:

– Will the digital textbook become more than a CD-ROM of the print version?
– How might the concept of the textbook change, if it becomes digital?
– How can digital textbooks to be developed as online digital textbooks?
– Are students mere consumers of digital content?

User interface design of digital textbooks exposes a wide variety of new possibilities, like interactive communication. A generalised suspension is an as unhelpful thing as the through assumption that universal design principles for all digital textbooks' interfaces are unequivocally good. To reflect on this issue let us analyse the evolution of web affordability for education.

A settled range of binaries reinforces this kind of assumption:

– Web 1.0 and education 1.0;
– Web 2.0 and education 2.0;
– Web 3.0 and education 3.0.

User interface design of textbook is repeatedly re-invented. Thus, if the web 1.0 is for web pages connected by hyperlinks, digital textbooks content are only static with hyperlinks; if the web 2.0 is for usability and interoperability, digital textbooks are embodied social media. In comparison with education 1.0 and education 2.0, user interface design of textbooks is for teacher-centered learning environment or learner-centered learning environment.

Education 2.0, known as 'social participatory web' enables students to participate actively in knowledge construction and dissemination. For the first time user interfaces were open for group and collaborative assessment and international projects. Instead of polarisation between web technology and learning theory, the educational methodology restricts sustained reflection on the complex nature of the user interface design in regard of innovation. Therefore, core principles of education 2.0 is active production, collaboration, sharing, publishing and social bookmarking. Even teachers and textbooks, both print or digital/digitized, are the main sources of knowledge, only the pioneers' teachers starting to adopt new functions and roles, like guides, mentors and coaches.

The actual phase of the digital revolution, characterised by cloud computing and 3.0 education, contributes on internationalisation of education for a sustainable development of each student in a globalised world. This is a fast-evolving phenomenon affecting all systems, environments, learning theory, strategies, and user-interface design of digital textbooks and, not in the last, the students' preferences for learning. Firstly, *cloud computing* creates on demand self-service, broad network access, resource pooling, rapid elasticity and measured service, which a common for an open digital world. Secondly, in a digital world the educational system with a learning environment is a holistic one, because the amount of the digital information increases tenfold every five years. Thirdly, education 3.0 is an umbrella term for many innovative technologies affordable for learning.

Living a life immersed in an open digital world has become part of the everyday human's activities. Technologies for education 3.0 are very different: from the philosophy of learning in a digital world to 3D Projector, educational ecosystems and interactive whiteboards implemented widely in schools since 2010. Thus, according to Texas Instruments (2016), using projectors make any surface in the classroom interactive, allowing an immersive experience that helps teachers teach and students learn. Project onto existing projector screens or whiteboards or directly anywhere the wall. By using a special pen, the teacher and/or the students can draw, can point and can click by touching the screen directly or from many feet away from the screen. These special features allow to interact with the entire screen no matter how large because the pen interacts from a distance or by touching the screen, as well as to control the students' activity in the classroom.

Education 3.0 will be impossible withhold the rapid development in e-paper and e-ink technologies. Heikenfeld (2011) has emphasized the rapid evolution of the e-paper technology with a flexible structure in the following abstract: 'the commercial success of monochrome electronic paper (e-paper) is now propelling the development of next-generation flexible, video, and color e-paper products. Unlike the early battles in the 1980s and 1990s between transmissive and emissive display technologies, there is an extraordinary diversity of technologies vying to become the next generation of e-paper.'

Now, more than ever, is needed a sustained reflection on the open digital world affordability for education. There are two distinctive feature of the digital world: (a) *mobile learning* and (b) education 3.0. In general, the mobile learning refers on ability to obtain or provide educational content on personal pocket devices such as PDAs, smartphones and mobile phones. According to Keats and Schmidt (2007), education 3.0 refers on rich, cross-institutional, cross-cultural opportunities within which the learners themselves play a key role as creator of knowledge *artifacts* that are shared, the distinction between artifacts, process and process becomes blurred as do distinction of space and time. In the 3.0 education, boundaries between teachers and students are breakdown and the social networking and social benefits outside the immediate scope of activity play a strong role.

At the current stage of the digital revolution, 50 % of knowledge occurs via *apps*. The most popular photo and video through WhatsApp or Social Media have shared, instead of the meeting in person. An evident fact is shifting the communication model from transmission to participative and self-directed learning. However, critical thinking regarding education 3.0 movement shows an evidence for a new frontier pedagogy, even some teachers advocate the classical approach in teaching, when textbooks is just a content for reading.

Education 3.0 is an indicator of living in a *digital society*, in, which 90 % of peoples said that smartphones never live their sides. Smartphones have a big potential for learning, e.g. it can be used to provide content just at the right time and just at the right place. Digital textbooks are in online education because of lower cost and flexibility. However, user generated content caused the knowledge sharing —skills based education. Thus, double model proposed for Education 3.0 is a proof to a movement toward viable competence pedagogy.

Three other important technologies, which may be included in the content of digital textbooks, are gamification, internet of things (IoT) and Big Data. Daggett (2015) notes that *gamification* is an important thing for learning. Incorporating gamification in a digital textbook allows developing an adoptive learning experience and skills. The most relevant gamification elements, which may be included in the content of the digital textbook, are rewards, feedback, rankings and exchanges. Indeed, their application for learning may motivate students through engagement, adaptively and interactivity. On the other side, IoT and Big Data are two of the most-talked-about technology topics in recent years.

However, according to Gartner's 2014 Hype Cycle for Emerging Technologies, the digital society is at the stage of *digital marketing* and sees the emergence of the *Nexus of Forces* (mobile, social, cloud and information). The next post-Nexus stage will be Digital Business, focused on the convergence of people, business and things. The IoT and the concept the physical and virtual worlds are strong concepts in this stage. The final post-Nexus paradigm name is Antonomous. For this stage is characterised an enterprise's ability to leverage technologies that provide humanlike or human-replacing capabilities.

Digital textbooks need an affordable user-interface design. In recent years, the theme of user interface design for digital textbooks have gathered significant attention by the scientific community, once it aims to solve one of the biggest problems that arises when using digital devices to reason knowledge provided by curriculum. Stansbury (2016) observed that the open courseware, open educational resources and adaptive/personalised learning are challenging the traditional model of course content creation and distribution (faculty-authored and publisher-produced textbooks). Personalisation and analytics are features in digital textbooks. However, less than half (45 percent) of the faculty surveyed in the ICBA and CCS report agreed/strongly agreed that digital course materials provide significant added value content not available in print.

In order to solve the issues of the significant added value of the digital textbooks, the most appropriate way is to facilitate the students' motivation to learn, explaining first of all, in which society they willlive, what competence (e.g. knowledge, skills, attitudes) is required for this society and why is important to contribute in a personal way for sustainable world.

Digital textbooks interfaces are designed both for knowledge (e.g. pedagogical resource) and skills development (e.g. learning tool). How important is to integrate digital textbooks in a knowledge management systems, distance education or is massive open online courses (MOOC)? It is important, if focus is learning, which in terms of 'education 3.0' defines a metasystem of independent, collaborative, dynamic and flexible self-regulated processes.

What is the impact of digital screens on self-regulated learning? Education 3.0 is a paradigm of thinking in complexity. Indeed, instructional systems, knowledge management systems or MOOC are complex systems and theirs functionality depends on the vitality of all elements 'working' together in linear or/and non-linear ways. However, as was written in the Ciller's book 'Complexity and postmodernism', the complex systems are constructed by a large number of elements, interacting richly, locally and non-linearly, containing feedback loops and being far from equilibrium. And learning is not only about the mechanical systems, but also about the changing in human's behaviour. This means that learning occurs, at least between two metasystems with a big entropy. However, the interface design of knowledge management systems is focused only on developing the ergonomic interfaces, and not on ecological learning. In the ecological learning students' cognitive systems should have developed the ecological features to 'connect' to various complex systems via vital (active) nodes.

1.3 Fourth Industrial Revolution and Education

The fourth industrial revolution is on the way: digital devices and software serves the teacher(s) and students activities to be networking engaged in various learning environments. The rationality for paradigm shift in the education was set out in the UNESCO Agenda, particularly in the goals for the sustainable development. Effectively, the objective of education has been redefined from *development of knowledge* to *sustainable development of competence*, as well as from the open and distributive environments to innovative application of technology to achieve sustainable development. These objectives have been endorsed as a competence development objective and, since that moment, this aim refers on the vital integrity of the knowledge, skills and attitudes for sustainable development.

However, only the education methodology is not in a position to deliver on these new objectives, having fallen behind social expectations since the educational crises of eighties-nineties. Next twenty years with some expectations to improve the education at the global level were affected, from the one hand, by the climate changes and, from the other hand, by major and observable trends toward 'intellectual' games, discovery of 'changing' synapses and others; most university teaching is still about the theories of antiquity philosophers, not about the current philosophical paradigms.

One of the core inventions of the fourth industrial revolution for education is *transhumanism*. According to Sorgner (2009), the transhumanism is in favour of technologies and other means, which could be used for enhancement of human intellectual, physical and emotional capacities. Thus, the philosophy has failed to acknowledge that the human society are practicing a sustainable strategy to adaptation in dynamic, not static circumstances, driven by Education 2030 agenda, adopted at the 70th Session of the United Nations General Assembly.

Educational philosophy is familiar with lead time, but this applies in regard to transhumanism; embodied cognition and energy saving educational technologies. Thus, the educational philosophy at the level of 4th industrial revolution integrates transhumanism with the knowledge of B-formatted representation in the brain, body's anatomy, higher order cognition and thinking, the extended mind hypothesis and the sensory-motor contingencies (Fig. 1.2).

This time digital textbooks interface design is at the level of the graphical design. However, from the philosophical point of view there is a significant impact of technological and scientific developments on the evolution of human species. But, these is only fresh berries in the old wine. According to Aksenov and Acsenov (2016), the aim of the philosophical concept of transhumanism is to liberate the human race from the inherent biological limitations. Education today depleting the cognition to be phased out, and the global challenges debate regarding the sustainable education with large implications for educational policy.

Learning designers would be insisting that the digital textbooks, as a pedagogical resource and as learning tool, are fully investigated and, will look critically at the potential of the digital textbook to develop the students' self-regulated learning strategies. By that time the generating costs of non-affective technologies for digital learning will be competitive with the generating costs of older technologies. The design of ecological user interfaces will be required by the open educational system as a matter of openness. Re-use of learning objects, even in open textbooks and eTextbooks, will be moved into more applications that are practical. Teacher(s) and students will routinely use metadata from databases,

Fig. 1.2 The lead time of the educational philosophy

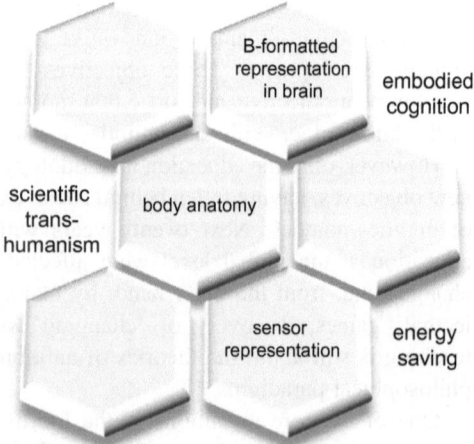

clouds and networks, which are accessible worldwide. Therefore, the fourth industrial revolution has accelerated the self-regulated strategy, but, also, re-opened the issue of metacognition and metacognitive strategies.

1.4 Open Educational System Versus Closed Pedagogical Systems

One of the impacts of digital revolution on learning refers on educational systems movement toward "much more open and flexible" (Frick 1991). Openness affects the content of school textbook and, therefore, changes standards for learning environment, tools and outcomes. In an open system, the learning process is less instructive, but more dynamic and flexible. Student become a *life-long learner* and, as a result, his/her capacity and motivation depends on many external factors, like social, technological, emotional and others. An example of the external technological factor is the possibility to read textbooks via Internet. Therefore, education 3.0 is an innovative model of a *distributed learning*.

An open educational system is a holistic whole with its environment or/and surroundings in forms of sharing *information* (data, knowledge), *energy* (skills, efforts and competences of life-long learners) and *intellect* (teachers, students, administrative and academic staff). Generally, the environment serves as the medium to convey the information from one source to other, but additional processes carry out the process of conveying the information. One of these complex processes is learning. However, learning requires energy. The energy conversion during digital learning is an issue that need urgent investigation.

During learning process the information and communication flows may take up a material form or/and a digital (quantum) form. Therefore, an important task for the learning designers is to understand the complex mechanism of perception the data from the screen. In plus, the data, information and knowledge is transferring in a dynamic and flexible way, 'changing' nature of competence pedagogy, in particular when data is transferred from digital to child's eyes/ears and vice versa, through touch screen, haptic and other technologies.

An open educational system manages complex mechanisms of data based on information/communication processes, cognitive activity processes and assessment processes. All these mechanisms and processes interconnect with the human body energy and power, stored and proving in the performance to learn and to make relevant decisions. Thus, taking into account that human body is also an open system, it can be understood why is learning is important to "holds" a real learning environment of open/closed systems with all multi-dimensional and multi-tasking mechanisms and processes. This means that learning with textbooks, instead of comprehensive reading, requires self-planning, self-regulation, self-directed and self-assessment techniques as a holistic strategy within lifelong learning.

Many countries promote the concept of lifelong learning. However, any strategy for the lifelong learning is affecting by some perturbation effects, which may influence memorization, attention, thinking, problem solving and decision-making. An example of the perturbation effects for learning is planning 'wrong' activities. To avoid this, is important to understand differences between open and closed, as well as between all components involved in learning. This is to say that before education 3.0 learning was planning as activities in a didactic system, which is part of the pedagogical systems (e.g. an artificial designed system with the scope of education or/and instruction). In such system, the instructional process has linear/systematic mechanisms within an instructional design model, incorporated into curricula. The teacher uses screen for teaching.

Vice Versa, learning in an open educational system is self-regulated. In such environment, the digital screen is for teaching, learning and assessment. This mode may be affordable, if in is designed an open system with an ecological (sustainable) environment and toward a sustainable development of a lifelong learner. For example, an open source textbook may have a content available for reading on screen, but only the student(s) can manage the accessibility for them. Thus, understanding and solving of user interface issues in digital textbooks use and development will make learning more controllable and adaptable.

The most important distinctions are between teacher-cantered and student-cantered learning environments. In teacher-cantered learning environments, digital textbooks are pedagogical resources, but in learner-cantered environments—learning tools. However, only an open source textbook provides the continuous supply of the potential energy that with the summative assessment tests not depleted. In plus, this energy by self-assessment may be increased. Therefore, the student learns when is motivated enough and has sufficient energy to avoid the negative feedback. The mechanism of own learning strategy depends of student's capacity to apply the metacognitive strategies for sustainable learning outcomes.

1.5   Toward Understanding the Terminology and Diversity of Digital Textbooks

Didactic revolution leads also to needs of experimentation a big diversity of digital textbooks, much more than for the printed textbooks. Some digital textbooks are still stored on CD-DVD or on computer. The cloud computing is a another way, which allow storing digital/digitised textbooks in cloud, as well as accessing digital textbooks via computer(s) and/or digital devices and reading them on digital screen or/and in a printed version. In a similar fashion, each textbook may be stored in a cloud *digital library*. Thus, everybody can develop own library of the digital textbooks and keep in three ways.

The personal library with digital textbooks anytime and anywhere is open. We can bring the cloud library with us, if use a digital device connected to Internet. In this library, textbooks can be digital/digitalized and include special learning algorithms. Compared with printed textbooks, digital textbooks have additional features, which allow users to take notes, highlight words, search words or topics, send or update information etc. Therefore, digital textbooks provides an increasing usability for achievement learning objectives.

Nevertheless, the most studied are monographic textbooks, which are developed through

– digitizing the existing printed textbooks;
– programing the content or instructional and/or assessment frameworks;
– personalisation of the open source content;
– development of own digital textbooks using authoring tools etc.

In the broadest sense, monographic digital textbooks can be classified in the following categories: (a) *eTextbooks*, which represents a subset of e-books; (b) *Open Source Textbooks*—open content and no restrictions on copying or printing and (c) *Cognitive Tutors*—intelligent solutions for understanding chemistry, biology, physics or foreign languages.

Open digital textbooks are developed under the terms of the GNU Free Documentation License. Such textbooks can be purchased or rented at a cost, or/and read online. eTextbooks have a variety of forms and models, even in an open or cloud format. Thus, as generic term, eTextbook (variously, electronic textbook, digital textbooks, e-book, iBook, Active Textbook, Interactive Textbook, Dynamic Book, a digital book, e-edition etc.) is an innovative textbook publication consisting of text, images, animation and multimedia, readable on computers, dedicated e-readers or other digital devices like tablets or smartphones. eTextbooks may have or not any printed equivalent. Instead, Open Source Textbooks (variously: Open Textbook, Free Online Textbook etc.) are online downloaded on to Personal Digital Assistance (PDA) or in a printed version at a low cost.

Modern digital technology, stored in the Internet, offers textbook delivery 24 h a day to any place in the world with Internet access. Once digital textbooks is accessed, the users can use a variety of opportunities to search information into the content by keywords; to understand the meaning of some words, to change text size in order to suit reader needs; to access hyperlinks to relevant external web pages, as required in content.

A Cognitive Tutor (variously: Intelligent Tutor, Adaptive Tutor etc.) is a particular kind of intelligent tutoring systems that utilizes *a cognitive model* to provide feedback to students as they are working through problems. Cognitive Tutor Authoring Tools are the special designed software for learning science, designers, and online course developers.

Digital textbooks in different *formats* are developed. The most used are PDF and open-source formats. The standard open-source format is ePub, more superior then PDF because ePub allows the text to be reflowed or resided according to size of digital device, giving a "side to side" digital reading experience. However, the ePub format requires using special eReading device or have downloaded and installed eReader software on the digital device. Users of Amazon Kindle or Amazon Kindle software use the MOBI format or download the special designed apps. The app is the abbreviation of world "application"—a special software program designed to fulfil a specific purpose, in particular, when is downloaded by a user to a mobile device. It can run on Internet, or on a mobile device.

Digital textbooks are available via a standard web browser. In the most cases teachers uses a HTML web site to distribute the textbook to students. The open format of HTML may allow users to edit or customize the textbook's content. In addition, can be created a zip file of textbook and make this file available for other instructors to download, edit or to host of other websites. When digital textbook is in a PDF format, the user should have a PDF reader, like Adobe Reader, Foxit and Nitro. Usually teachers distributes academic textbooks in PDF format for reading. Students can read the content online or print the provided content. However, in a collaborative project a teacher can make the content available for comments.

The other, less used formats are doc., docx and .html. These formats require a Microsoft Word are a source compatible with Word, such as OpenOffice or Google Text. These formats as a source file for those who want to edit or to add content, usually in a collaborative project are used. In some special cases, for a complex scientific equations and notations, are required LaTeX. Therefore, in the tradition of Herbard, a Didaktik triangle is a key tool for analysing the complex relations between teacher T, student S and content C. The complex relations between T, S and C should be treated as a whole, in case when the starting point is the *pedagogical communication* between the teacher T and the student(s) S. The pedagogical communication is a term common in teacher-cantered learning environments, used to define the ability of teacher to communicate knowledge and to facilitate understanding.

After digital revolution, the teachers' functions "*to teach*" has changed. Individual pedagogical approach is moved to Participatory Learning and Action (PLA) approach, i.e. learning "about and engaging with communities" (Thomas 2016, p. 1). This approach, used in identified needs, planning, monitoring or evaluating projects and programmes, combines an ever-growing toolkit of participatory and visual methods with natural interviewing techniques and is intended to facilitate a process of collective analysis and learning.

As part of the global technological challenges, the need of getting diploma in a "local" University is not important. The diversity of digital learning environments with the emerging e-books, digital textbooks, open sources, social media, MOOC and mobile technologies have forever changed the local landscape of the formal schooling with a two-directed pedagogical communications model. We now live in a real and virtual, local and global learning environment in which knowledge twice every days is increased. Icons in their mobile devices drive the students outside of their digital screens. So what this mean for Didactic triangle?

"Combining" learning theory, learning strategies, textbook theory and participatory approach to self-regulated learning in a digital world opens the door to powerful new successful educational methodologies that may result in documented benefits for students. Instead, to realize these strategies teachers need support in understanding how digital screen affects learning. On the one hand, a participative approach involves solving real problems based on the active participation in the self-regulated learning process; on the other hand, this require an innovative pedagogical relation between the student and the teacher(s). Therefore, in considering the interdependencies between both the teacher and student the preferred term is "learning". One can observe that this is a new didactic relation, which include technology as a norm. The teacher's key task in this new didactic relation is to guide the learning process of the student from start to success in life.

The goal of user interface design is to anticipate the moment of positive responses on tasks provided according to provided content. Students construct knowledge through gathering and synthesizing information and integrating it with the general skills of inquiry, communication, critical thinking, problem solving and so on. Learning design norms require cognitive ergonomics, learning needs, self-regulated strategies, dynamics, analytics and styles. In such environments students work alone or in pairs and small groups on theirs papers, projects, portfolios and other. Teaching and assessing is intertwined. Therefore, the goal of the user interface design is to involve students in learning process. There are specific principles and norms for learning design in a Global Age. Professor and students learn together. The common feature of learning is metacognitive strategies.

When considering their teaching and assessment approaches, class development strategy or method to instruction, teachers are always looking for the way that is most beneficial for all of their students. Teachers want their students to understand the topic, to communicate and to collaborate on provided tasks. As a result, the debate of teacher-cantered vs. learner-cantered learning environment has been in the forefront of learning designers' minds.

Regarding the user interface design there are controversial opinions, too. These controversies, indeed, comes from the contradictions between learning theory and design of the *learning objects* toward developing a learning construct, from one part, and chaos theory and proactivity of open system learning environments, from the other. This means that a classical didactic triangle has been changing (Fig. 1.3).

The diversity of the learning environments, which, as was pointed by (Midoro 2005, p. 42) are global and local, real and virtual, directly affect the didactic triangle. This means that students are not only receiver the content and learn not only in school. The open content for learning can be taking into consideration as an independent point, as well as the context of learning. By context for learn we understand *the ability for a learning object to interconnect various, similar events or statements* (Downes 2004). Therefore, this global reality of the globalised educational systems

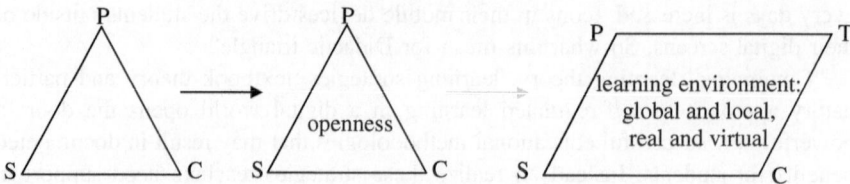

Fig. 1.3 Transforming the didactic triangle into the didactic tetrahedron (where P-professor, S-student, C-content, T-digital textbook as a context for learning)

with/and various environments evidence many uncertainties embedded in ill-structured problems, related on student, teacher, content and context for learning. These problems are the heart of the contemporary learning science.

References

Aksenov, I. V., & Аксёнов, И. В. (2016). Trans-humanism as an anthropological problem. *Journal of Siberian Federal University*, Humanities and Social Sciences, *3*(9), 678–686.

Aleksander, I. (1970). Some psychological properties of digital learning nets. *International Journal of Man-Machine Studies, 2*(2), 189–212.

Aleksander, I. (1975). Action-oriented learning networks. *Kybernetes, 4*(1), 39–44.

Aleksander, I., & Stonham, T. J. (1979). Guide to pattern recognition using random-access memories. *IEE Journal on Computers and Digital Techniques, 2*(1), 29–40.

Bandura, A. (1977). Social learning theory. http://www.esludwig.com/uploads/2/6/1/0/26105457/bandura_sociallearningtheory.pdf

Bloom, B. S. (1956). *Taxonomy of educational objectives: The classification of educational goals.* Harlow, Essex, England: Longman Group.

Brusilovsky, P., Schwarz, E., & Weber, G. (2003). Electronic textbooks on WWW: From static hypertext to interactivity and adaptivity. In B. H. Khan (Ed.), *Web-based instruction* (pp. 255–261). Englewood Cliffs, New Jersey: Educational Technology Publications. http://www.pitt.edu/~peterb/papers/Badrul.html

Coulson, J. E., & Cogswell, J. F. (1965). Effects of individualized instruction on testing. *Journal of Educational Measurement, 2*(1), 59–64.

Coyle et al. (2016). Reducing click distance through social adaptive interfacing. https://www.researchgate.net/publication/230875702_Reducing_Click-Distance_through_Social_Adaptive_Interfacing

Daggett, W. R. (2015). *Preparing students for their future.* International Center for Leadership in Education. http://www.leadered.com/PP/Midway,%20UT%209.10.2015.pdf

Digital vs Digitized Learning. https://byotnetwork.com/2015/09/08/digital-vs-digitized-learning/

Downes, S. (2004). What is a learning context? http://www.downes.ca/post/18

Elio, R., & Anderson, J. R. (1984). The effects of information order and learning mode on schema abstraction. *Memory & Cognition, 12*(1), 20–30.

Fisher, R. B., & Koryllos, K. (1998). Interactive textbooks; embedding image processing operator demonstrations in text. *International Journal of Pattern Recognition and Artificial Intelligence, 12*(08), 1095–1123.

Frick, T. W. (1991). *Restructuring education through technology.* Bloomington, Indiana: Phi Delta Kappa Educational Foundation. https://www.indiana.edu/~tedfrick/fastback/fastback326.html/ Accessed April 05, 2016

Gagne, R. (1985). The conditions of learning, 4th. edn. New York: Holt, Rinehart & Winston.

Gartner, J. (2016). Gartner's 2014 hype cycle for emerging technologies maps the journey to digital business. http://www.gartner.com/newsroom/id/2819918

Glaser, R. (1962). Psychology and Instructional Technology. Training Research and Education. In R. Glaser, (Ed.), Pittsburgh: University of Pittsburgh Press.

Greenfield, J. (2013). Students, professors still not yet ready for digital textbooks. *Digital Book World.* http://www.digitalbookworld.com/2013/students-professors-still-not-yet-ready-for-digital-textbooks/

Hathaway, M. D. (1984). Variables of computer screen display and how they affect learning. *Educational Technology, 24*(1), 7–11.

Heikenfeld, J. (2011). A critical review of the present and future prospects for electronic paper. Journal of the Society for Information Display, *19*, 129. doi:10.1889/JSID19.2.129

Howard, J. (2013). For many students, print is still king. *Chronicle of Higher Education.* http://chronicle.com/article/For-Many-Students-Print-Is/136829/

Kaplan, J. M. (2015). Race, IQ, and the search for statistical signals associated with so-called "X"-factors: environments, racism, and the "hereditarian hypothesis". *Biology & Philosophy, 30*(1), 1–17. doi:10.1007/s10539-014-9428-0

Keats, D., & Schmidt, J. P. (2007). Three generations of education. *12*(3). http://firstmonday.org/ojs/index.php/fm/article/view/1625/1540#k2

Knowles, M. S. (1975). *Self-directed learning.* Cambridge Adult Education. http://www.strategiesforabetterway.com/documents/augustbookreview.pdf

Lewin, D., & Lundie, D. (2016). Philosophies of digital pedagogy. Studies in Philosophy and Education, *35*(3), 235–240. 10.1007/s11217-016-9514-7, http://link.springer.com/article/10.1007/s11217-016-9514-7/fulltext.html

Lubow, R. E., Rifkin, B., & Alek, M. (1976). The context effect: The relationship between stimulus preexposure and environmental preexposure determines subsequent learning. *Journal of Experimental Psychology: Animal Behavior Processes*, *2*(1), 38–47. https://www.researchgate.net/profile/Robert_Lubow/publication/232430122_The_context_effect_The_relationship_between_stimulus_preexposure_and_environmental_preexposure_determines_subsequent_learning/links/004635379a8c8af01b000000.pdf

Midoro, W. (2005). A common European framework for teachers' professional profile in ICT for education. Ortona, Italy: Edizioni Menabo Didactica.

Morrarty, E. (2013). Webcast: The digital revolution in higher education: Attitudes on e-textbooks and more. http://www.digitalbookworld.com/2013/webcast-the-digital-revolution-in-higher-education-attitudes-on-e-textbooks-and-more/

Plowman, L. (2016). Learning technology at home and preschool. *The Wiley Handbook of Learning Technology*, 96–112.

Project Gutenberg Mission Statement by Michael Hart. http://www.gutenberg.org/wiki/Gutenberg:Project_Gutenberg_Mission_Statement_by_Michael_Hart

Schwarz, E., Brusilovsky, P., & Weber, G. (2005). World-wide intelligent textbooks. *i-Manager's Journal of Educational Technology, 1*(4), 23.

Shiffrin, R. M., & Schneider, W. (1977). Controlled and automatic human information processing: II. Perceptual learning, automatic attending and a general theory. *Psychological Review, 84*(2), 127–139.

Skinner, B. F. (1954). *The science of learning and the art of teaching* (pp. 99–113). Cambridge, Mass, USA.

Smith, R. (2000). The purpose, design, and evolution of online interactive textbooks: the digital learning interactive model. *History Computer Review, 16*(2), 43.

Sorgner, S. L. (2009). Nietzsche, the overhuman, and transhumanism. *Journal of Evolution and Technology, 20*(1), 29–42.

Stansbury, M. (2016). The future of textbooks look like this. http://www.ecampusnews.com/top-news/digital-textbooks-faculty-177/

Stiegler, B. (2016). The digital, education, and cosmopolitanism. *Representations, 134*(1), 157–164.

Stonham, T. J., & Shaw, M. A. (1975). Automatic classification of mass spectra by means of digital learning nets-existence of characteristic features of chemical class in mass spectra. *Pattern Recognition, 7*(4), 235–241.

Texas Instruments (2016). Interactive projectors. http://www.ti.com/lsds/ti/dlp-technology/products/dlp-projectors/interactive-projector.page

The future of the electronic paper. http://thefutureofthings.com/3081-the-future-of-electronic-paper/

Thomas, S. (2016). What is Participatory Learning and Action (PLA): An Introduction. http://idp-key-resources.org/documents/0000/d04267/000.pdf

Wright, J., & Mischel, W. (1982). Influence of affect on cognitive social learning person variables. *Journal of Personality and Social Psychology, 43*(5), 901.

Zinn, K. L. (1967). Computer technology for teaching and research on instruction. *Review of Educational Research, 37*(5), 618–634.

Клир Д. (1990). Системология. Автоматизация решения системных задач. Москва: Радио и связь. 538 с.

Chapter 2
A Paradigm Shifths and User Interface Design Models

A new type of thinking is essential if mankind to survive and move toward higher levels.

Albert Einstein

Abstract A paradigm shifts, according to Thomas Kuhn, is a fundamental change in the basic concepts and experimental practices of a scientific discipline. Do paradigm shifts change the design models according to changes in education? The goal of this chapter is to present a comprehensive description of linear, systems and meta-systems thinking approaches. Its scope is limited to the instructional design models and principles of user interface design. The chapter deeply explores the contrasts, connections, and influences from the realm of thinking to the real.

Keywords Linear thinking · Systemic thinking · Metasystem thinking

2.1 Introduction

The term 'design' may be associated with the thinking' patterns. According to Visser (2006), design thinking is the design-specific cognitive activities that designers apply during the process of designing. But, can be only the cognitive activities important for instructional design? Let us analyse this idea starting from the paradigm shifts in education. The term 'paradigm shift', coined by the Thomas Kuhn, defines a fundamental change in the basic concepts and experimental practice of a scientific discipline. In the case of the digital textbook theory and design, the paradigm shifts could be associated with education 1.0, education 2.0 and education 3.0 and, therefore, with changes in the intellectual inquiry noted in the educational technology as well as in philosophy, psychology, cybernetics, and neuroscience and knowledge management.

Hairston (1982, pp. 78–80) notes that to understand the nature of the paradigm shift in textbooks' development is important to look at the principal features of that educational paradigm that has been the basis of the composition teaching for several decades or hundreds of years, taking into account that textbooks' police and content

© Springer Nature Singapore Pte Ltd. 2017   23
E.A. Railean, *User Interface Design of Digital Textbooks*,
Lecture Notes in Educational Technology, DOI 10.1007/978-981-10-2456-6_2

change slowly. Publishers want to keep what sells, and they tend to direct the appeals of their books to what they believe the average composition teacher wants, not to what those in the vanguard of the profession would like to have. In turn, for them is better to accept the digitalised version of printed textbook that to implement a new interactive technology, even this technology is better for learning.

Nevertheless, the big changes in textbook theory and design are under way. Following the patterns that Kuhn describes in his theory, the first response to crisis in education has been to improvise the individualised learning through programmed instruction. Among the first response were teaching machine and programed textbook, which sprang up about 50–70 years ago to give first aid to teachers who seemed unable to teach students within the traditional paradigm.

However, the first attempt has not solved the problem. Another ad hoc 'problem solving' within self-directed learning and local networking in classroom, but, as was it noted by Hairston (1982, p. 82), it has faded from the scene along with the computer-assisted instruction. In plus, network and cloud computing, nano-education and big data, common for education 3.0, are the actual ad hoc measure that paradigm is only a temporally palliative for problems related on sustainable education. Not all have solved the crisis of education. What are the reasons?

In our point of view, any paradigm is only the background for solving common controversies, problems or issue. More important is to develop and to implement a theory with well-defined principles that will correlate with the paradigm. What we have today in user interface design of digital textbooks is inexplicable, on the one hand, education 3.0 and on the other hand, design principles based on learning theories for XV–XIX century.

Among the solutions of reconceptualisation the user interface design of digital textbooks, one of them is design thinking—a mindset as the strategy of innovation in learning. However, in this case the user interface design must be updated at the level of accepted paradigm. What we have today? As was noted by Teal (2010, p. 295), most students appear to undertake the process of design in a more or less linear fashion. This practice is exemplified in the oft heard phrase, 'I would have done "X" if I'd only had enough time …', which is frequently employed to explain why site development, detailing, materials—in short, things associated with a 'finished' building—are left unattended. Could be the linear design thinking so problematic for learning?

Systems thinking is, according to Richmond (1994) 'the art and science of making reliable inferences about behavior by developing an increasingly deep understanding of underlying structure'. The author find many differences which allow to say that system thinking is not similar with General Systems Theory, not it is System analyses, Chaos Theory, Dissipative Structures, Operations Research, Decision Analysis, or Systems' Dynamics. Thus, systems thinking enable to develop special thinking skills, characterised by the term 'bi-focal'. People embracing systems thinking filters can see both the forest and the tree in three ways: system as cause thinking, closed-loop thinking and operational thinking. The most important thing of this theory is that operational thinking viewed with the framework of system dynamics.

There is a widespread though controversial belief about the fact that digital textbooks design is shaped according to the humans' thinking paradigms regarding the artificial systems. Perhaps more importantly, the pre-eminence of the work perpetuates the criteria, which asserts that world produced only a limited number of thinking patterns—hence a competition for an affordable digital textbook user interface design really exists. Does is it mean that design thinking models are most at the philosophical or theoretical stakes, therefore, the instructional designers are not able to use them? Or, maybe, the digital textbooks are only the youngest brothers of the printed textbooks and, therefore, the user interface design is not an issue?

2.2 User Interfaces Issues in Digital Textbooks Use and Development

Human thinking paradigm is a common way to understand user interfaces patterns in digital textbooks use and development. Once we believe that competence is the power of the adaptive living in the actual world, the user interface design should allow developing digital skills, like digital reading, listening online or sharing content. Does these ways are the best to replace printed textbooks with digital versions? From the one hand, research has shown that students understand text less whey they read on computers.

> When reading on screens, for example, people seem to reflexively skim the surface of texts in search of specific information, rather than dive in deeply in order to draw inferences, construct complex arguments, or make connections to their own experiences. Research has also found that students, when reading digitally, tend to discard familiar print-based strategies for boosting comprehension (Montuori 2012).

Listening online is a good way to learn, for example, a foreign language. Instead of the printed textbooks, digital textbooks may offer digital listening, reading and vocabulary practice. Audio textbooks for music education may include audio recording of famous artists as well as practical exercises. However, user interfaces of digital textbooks could allow students to assessable own textbooks, including own audio recordings or video. These are two different approaches: teacher centered and learner—centered. In is more than rationale to combine both approaches within learning, but there are two ways: *reproductive learning* and *productive learning*. Thus,

> Reproductive Learning is an umbrella term for a form of education based on rote memorization and reproduction of existing knowledge. It reproduces the content, process, social structures, power relations, and individuals that conform to what are perceived to be societal needs and norms, mostly derived from the need to train workers at various levels of expertise. It is often the result if not the actual goal of educational approaches centered on assessment, and where the acquisition of existing information and conceptual frameworks is central. The learner and his/her values, experience, affect, and ultimately identity are not included in the learning process. Creativity and, therefore, the original generation and application of information and conceptual frameworks are not valued (Montuori 2012, p. 2838)

Reproductive learning is about memorization. Therefore, both those who use teacher-centered approached with different levels of achievement and those who do not go beyond simple instructions like *memorise this* (in a teacher-centered learning environment), are right. That is not to claim that students who are attain classrooms only use simple instructions. They may memorise some things involuntary or voluntary within computer-based assessment environment.

Productive learning is about solving problem with insight. Therefore,

Productive Learning is learning on the basis of productive activity in social "serious situations", learning on the basis of experience, of being able to achieve something important, both for oneself and one's environment. Thus, young people feel themselves to be important and valuable members of society and not simply reduced to the status of a school pupil. Productive Learning begins with activity i.e. learning is itself a product gained by experience of productive activity and young people acquire this with the assistance of educationalists (INNEPS 2016, p. 1)

For decades, educational research indicates that learning is equal to memorisation. Education 3.0 changes this vision in favour of productive learning. Which models: productive or reproductive learning, are required for an affordable user interfaces of digital textbooks? Recently, the validity of the dichotomy between reproductive and productive learning has been questioned by the results of both qualitative and quantitative research, which demonstrated that successful learning depends on problem that students have or on issue that is proposed to be solved as well as what IQ is required or how many information and energy is required.

'User interface design of digital textbook means display mode and pattern of digital textbook's content and multimedia resource. The user interface design will not facilitate better easy operation if it does not meet users' needs' (Liu et al. 2014, p. 130). But, recently research demonstrated that designers could think about digital communication in qualitatively new way. For instance, following the idea of Pandea Communications, billions of peoples around the world will be connected online using a voice call. Therefore, soon everybody will be connected to Internet via a future phone or Android device, even they don't have a digital device. In sum, there are five communications patterns in design of user interfaces: text (message), picture (graphic), audio (voice), video (TV, multimedia), and touch (multi-touch).

The perception of affordance in user interface design for learning has been questioned by a phenomenon, which is generally referred to the paradox of the design thinking as a solution for innovation. This paradox introduces two stereotypes: *universal design for learning* and *personalised design for learning* (Karsvall 2002). The universal design aims to improve and optimize teaching and learning for all peoples based on *representation* (e.g. present information and content in different ways); *engagement* (e.g. stimulate interest and motivation for learning); *action and representation* (e.g. differentiate the ways that students can express what they know). This is a case of flexible curriculum and setting up the aims, objectives and methods, which work for everyone so that each student can progress.

The second stereotype introduces the term 'personalised design' and is principally based on the study how learning parts can be adapted to students' progress. However, in practice, it was developed some prototypes patterns, defined by

Karsvall (2002, p. 1), as neutral, extrovert and introvert design. The neutral design is equivalent to the original prototype: it display variations of saturated hues in greens, blues, reds, black and white and users both rounded and squared shapes. The extrovert prototype provides higher contrast between interactive elements and even more saturated red, yellow and blue hues as well as darken inactive areas. The introvert design was accordingly given lower contrasts and de-saturated colours in white, green and blue. These two stereotypes are incompatible as taken together they seem to suggest that only rote learning or active learning based on psycho-physiological characteristics of students leads to academic success.

The concept of *user interface design* is central to behavioural, cognitivist and constructivist approaches. Behavioural approach is more related on designing programmed textbooks, but cognitivist—on designing multimedia and interactive textbooks. Almost, the user interfaces designing multimedia interactive textbooks for learning is Instructional Systems Design models. Usually these models describe the principles either Merrill or Gagne theories, or provide an individual model, like ADDIE, Dick and Carey, Morrison, Ross and Kemp and others. This is why the requirements of how to generate data on screen are very different.

Moreover, required processing, analysing, synthesis and communication actions by students, as well as planning and development of instructional objectives by teachers on the base on provided information on screen presents a variety of challenges for designers of the digital textbooks. There are one big issue: abstract data. Thus, abstract data could be presented as metadata, structured information, multimedia, audio or graphic representation, or/and knowledge for feedback. There are multiple ways. One way is a user interface in which the immediate feedback 'follows' the content within tasks designed for individualised learning in order to make the provided content more understandable. The other way is user interface in which information presented on the screen serve only as metadata for personalised learning. The third way is the user interface, which present strictly individualised content, adapted to user's progress.

Consider, for example, that user interface design models evolves according to human thinking paradigms. Thus, Dick and Carey model was developed in 1990, during the second phase of the digital revolution. The model describes the design process in ten steps: identification the instructional aim, analysing the instructional aim, analysing the learner and the content, writing performance objectives, development of assessment methods, development of instructional strategy, development of instructional methods, design and development of formative assessment, control of programme' content and summative assessment.

The model of Morrison, Ross and Kemp was developed in 2004 (during the intermediary period between second and third phase!). This model describes the user interface design according to ADDIE scheme. Instead of the instructional aim, it is proposed to identify the *instructional problem* through evaluation of needs, analysing of aim, and evaluation of performance. The phase of analysing the instructional aim is changing with analysing of students and required tasks (general characteristics, competence, learning style, analysing of context). Moreover, writing the performance objectives, according to previous model, were changes in favour of instructional objectives and performance matrix. The stage 'development of instructional objectives' in completed with the dimension, succession, frequences of frames and instructional strategies. Assessment and control is completed with testing of knowledge, abilities, behavior and attitude.

In sum, all ADDIE instructional design models neglect the differences between the author vision of design' elements and the reader's perception. This subject has been discussed all times particularly because of the concerns that it raises as teacher, student and content, on one hand, are often wrongly used interchangeably. On other hand, it is neglected the changing context for learning. Thus, in the concept of education 3.0 students prefer to share knowledge instead of getting knowledge; to access the on-line courses in order to explore new subjects instead of listening lessons in classroom; 'external control' instead of formative/summative assessment.

Does above-mentioned features indicate at evolution of user interface design? In the classic model of education, text and picture communicates clearly the information to student through printed interfaces. Numerous design thinkers note that user interfaces of the student's textbook should differs from the user interface of teacher's textbook. Only teacher is able to establish connection between textbook and students' needs in learning.

An ideal visualisation should not only communicate clearly, but also stimulate viewer's engagement and gain attention to some elements (Viegas and Wattenberg 2011). What is threatening about emerging technologies are potential scenarios of life, according to scientific transhumanism, taking over the world, and bringing both humanism and trans-humanim approached into design of interfaces for the un-existed world. This approach displays abstract instead of real knowledge and without to develop any skills and attitudes.

In theory and practice, there are multiple ways how to design user interface design for better engagement in learning. However, all this ways are suitable within one specific period, and there are not only one unique way for all periods. That is why, for instructional designers and publishers of the first digital textbooks to believe that learning is both reproductive and productive is fine as long as they don't need to develop textbooks' models beyond parameters of the digitised version of traditional school textbooks for sustainable education. This is more than learner-centered learning environments and relate on learning philosophy.

The postmodernism philosophy requires that learners will explore artifacts and patterns from the real world and, therefore, that learner to be motivated enough to think about own thinking and how to develop own abilities. On the other hand, the rapid digitalisation of the educational systems requires that learner to become a lifelong learner in order to be able to explore different cultures and diversity of learning environments for the best decisions regarding the sustainable development. Therefore, understanding the specific characteristic of the period in which user interface will be used is the best way in design affordable textbooks.

Each paradigm of design has had its day. The paradigm of digital textbook changed the understanding of learning forever in three steps: linear, systems and metasystems. Thus, now learning can be understood well starting from the mindset of the human paradigm. For example, the humanistic paradigm has been the common belief for ages, but now Newtonian physics is at a loss when it needs to explain the quantum energy of thinking. Moreover, learner is not only human, but also a (meta)cognitive and affective system. Humans are "connected" through (meta)patterns bridges with all objects and subjects of real and virtual world. In brief, the user interface design of digital textbooks should be a real project aims to develop a well-defined learning mechanism.

2.3   Linear Thinking: Direct and Branching Styles

From the perspectives of changing paradigm of learning within digital revolution, 'linear thinking' is related to step-by-step progression when knowledge is assimilated in small steps. The learner must follow the 'path' presented by the programmer, however the learner using a programmed text may deviate from the path set down by the programmer by looking back in the program or looking ahead. One of the first example of linear thinking refers on user interface design of teaching machines. As was noted by Eigen (1962, p. 453):

> a teaching machine presents an ordered sequence of instruction to the learner one frame at a time. After responding to a stimulus frame, the learner's answer is immediately confirmed or corrected. The learner then proceed to the next frame; he is prevented from changing his previous answer or going back in the program. In a horizontal programmed text, succeeding frames appear on alternative pages. The learner write his answer to the frame either in the program booklet or on a separate answer sheet. He then turns the page, and the correct response is revealed along with the next stimulus frame. A horizontal text is read from the front of the book to the back, across the page, at one level. After completing the top level, the learner read across the text at the next lower level. This procedure is continued until the either text has been read. <...> Vertical programmed text are read from the top of the page to the bottom. The number of pages appeared on one page may vary from one to ten or twelve. A mask or slider is used with this mode of presentation.

For over 50 years, linear design of digital textbooks has embarked on numerous educational projects, but the obtained results are controversial. In brief, the linear designers prefer to understand learning as a stimulus-response or as a stimulus-response-reinforced associations, which allow developing a new behavior. During learning it is involved the dependent and independent variables. Thus, the dependent variable is a change in behavior that are observable and tangible. Instead, the independent variable is the consequence of behavior.

Smith and Smith (1966) have wrote, that learning is more than the open loop forming of new stimulus-response associations. Learning is a process of reorganization of sensory activity within a closed loop, or pattern, which is a process of reorganization of sensory feedback within a closed loop, or pattern, which increases the learner's level of control over his own behavior and the stimuli in his environment. Therefore, for these authors the learning is space-organized rather than time-organized activity, organised from simple to complex and it is dependent on the behavioural objectives and on design principles of the learning situation, especially the techniques and the instruments of education.

When learning is a space—organized activity, the school textbooks should follow curricula based on instructional (or behavioural) objectives. The objectives are realisable through individualized instruction with active practice and frequent feedback to students. For these objectives, in school textbooks should be included a simple-to-complex sequencing of content, criterion-referencing testing, self-pacing, mastery learning and much more. However, the linear designed content of textbooks is the fashion for Skinner's programmed textbooks.

Let us analyse deeper the linear thinking design of the programed textbook. A programmed textbook is a special designed program in the form of a textbook, which in addition to instructional material provides schemas of learning including reading/listening and control of knowledge assimilation. The principles of programed textbooks are clear learning objectives, small steps, logical sequence, active responding, and immediate feedback, drill and practice and stimulus fading. However, instead of the well-defined principals of reinforced learning, the lessons in computer classrooms were bored. What are the reasons?

Linear thinking is related to instructional design approach. The term 'instructional design' defines a technology for the development of learning experiences and environment, which promote the acquisition of specific knowledge and skills by students. On the other hand, the term *'instructional design'* defines the process of planning instruction, delivering instruction and assessing student in the classroom and a form of complex problem solving (Handani et al. 2011, pp. 1–2). However, this approach is described by a behavior-oriented model which insists that students have fixed abilities be learned.

There are two possible ways: direct style and branching style. Philosophically, according to Skinner's theory, the people learn better through direct observation using own senses and learning is based on tangible, observable and repeatable factors. The learning outcomes can be observed and recorded. After the instruction period (e.g. a semester), the learner should demonstrates a new behavior. How to do this with so various unconnected concepts proposed through curriculum, and various textbooks' design for one level students? The fact that students cannot learn science only in a computer class is an issue, which can be solved by re-conceptualisation of curricula, as well as of the setup of the textbook design.

From other point of view, linear thinking is a way of linear programing and, therefore, correlates with the first phase of the digital revolution. This phase relates both on *visual thinking*, e.g. idea-sketching, seeing, and imagining and *audiovisual thinking* (Schlesinger and Waelde 2011; Tchulkina and Garbar 2016; Flynn 2016). On other hand, linear thinking is associated with classical instructional design models with teacher-centered learning environment, even it was started the research in mathetics.

In the context of these ideas, the main concepts methodology within user interface design have shown to be lacking. Researchers and practitioners, working in interdisciplinary area of pedagogy, rethink digital textbook design on an expanded basic in line with sustainable education (Hjorth and Bagheri 2006;

Bosch and Nguyen 2016; Ha et al. 2016). Thus, as was noted by Ha et al. (2016, p. 1), development efforts through the traditional approach of linear thinking with tends to solve immediate (visible) problems in isolation without an understanding of the local contexts and participation of direct beneficiaries and related stakeholders that have posed many flaws, leading to failures and counterproductive outcomes.

The methodology of learning is simple: students read the content on screen and answer questions. However, the content should be read from beginning to end and all students should follows the same objectives. It is expected that all students are 'linear thinkers', i.e. have the capacity to proceed information in a sequential manner. The didactic process is predicable by instructional objectives, small frames on screen, questions, answers and guidelines. This model is not the best for the actual students who understand media in other way, no as a text or image in book or textbook but as the bound screens up with in complex ways and patterns.

In linear design the content "takes" the learner in a positive progress, which starts only with positive feedback, and then works through problem solving, understanding the concepts and reinforcement the results. This means that the event A (cause) leads to event B (effect), which leads to C, then leads to D etc., and when each step is guided by well-defined objectives. On a user interface can be seen the Stimulus 1 (S_1) that offer all conditions for Stimulus 2 (S_2) etc.

Various learning scenarios prove the efficiency of linear thinking. The first benefits are *memory improvement* and *second language acquisition*. However, these benefits cannot be archived through simple mechanisation of education. The "mechanization of education", as was observed by Skinner (1965), leads only to development of the computer-based teaching machine and of the mechanical teachers. But, "to automate education with mechanical teachers is like automating banking with mechanical tellers and bookkeepers" (p. 5).

Furthermore, Skinner (1965) observed that students might learn without teaching, but also, that only a teacher arranges conditions under which students learn more rapidly and effectively. The teacher begins with whatever behavior the student brings to the instructional situation; by selective reinforcement, he changes that behavior so that a given terminal performance is more and more closely approximated. The experimental analysis of behavior has more to contribute to a *technology of education*. This model describes *instrumental conditioning*. It was expected that the students' behavior can conveniently be mediated by mechanical devices when machines present material and differentially reinforce his responses.

Any practical application of knowledge about learning theory is, of course, *pedagogy*. However, according to linear thinking approach the pedagogy describes only a technique of processing a stimulus S and getting answer R within the provided content. Therefore, learning is distancing from the real *performance* of the learner. That is why; the linear thinking in design of digital textbook was changed through time by multiple ideas:

– to find better teachers;
– to set up model schools, staffed by model teachers;

- to simplify what is to be learned; to reorganize what is to be learned;
- to improve presentation techniques;
- to establish multiply contacts between teacher and students;
- to expand the educational system from local system to global network of school
- to raise educational standards.

It is the time to re-think user interface design of digital textbooks. The task of the teacher is to improve the students' skills. Nevertheless, whose of the thinking models is attributed this task? Skinner (1965, p. 15) wrote that mostly programmed instruction has been called "Socratic", because of small steps and leading through an argument with verbal prompts. The second way is Comenius who advocated breaking material into a large number of small steps, arranged in a plausible genetic order. However, these are not enough because the student should not proceed until will fully motivated to learn at a given stage.

Advocates of linear thinking (e.g. Benjamin 1988, p. 708) prove that student's success could be maximized and that errors could be kept to a near zero level. To ensure this kind of learning, the material had to be organized in a coherent fashion, building a response repertoire, step by tiny step. One of the example on digital screen is *programmed English*, presented by Joyce et al. (2000, p. 333).

1. Words are divided into classes. We

    call the largest class nouns. Nouns are
    a class of _____. words

2. In English the class of words called

    nouns is larger than all the other
    _____ of words combined classes

The problem is that until recently the most people had learn in a linear fashion, and, therefore, follows yet the linear patterns for own living. A linear pattern learning is said to exist when the initial and final points examined form a straight line. Thus, for them the learning starts with positive results from primary school and proceeds straight across to the high school to University. During teaching, the teacher fellows the curricula, starting from beginning and moving in a straight line to the end. He/she uses the textbook and presentation on screen. Screen is used for reading core ideas of content, writing in a logical manner, from simple to complex.

In a linear fashion, a didaktik problem is easy to be solved. All of the didaktik 'things', like the context for learning, content, environment, and instructional objectives are together. Nevertheless, this is not a holistic approach of learning, but only a linear thinking about how to design learning. People understand dimensions, consistence and hierarchy of instructional frames differently. In fact, linear thinking designers believe that they know how to solve problems of today learning, but in reality do not know how to design user interface design. There are many reasons.

Some students have good memory, and some not. Some students are be able to 'mentally divide' problems in frames, and some not. Other students need to write all frames on a digital screen in a copybook to understand the order of solving the provided tasks. They may need a tool able 'to translate' information into his/her *mode of perception*. Explaining problem solving on digital screen in a linear fashion does not help with this issue.

Branching programing or branching style of the linear thinking is a technique of learning with computer. On screen, each frame presents more text than the average linear frame. After reading, the user responds to a question, usually in a multiple-option format and may receive corrective feedback in order to remediate the learner's misconceptions or gaps in understanding. There are multiple approaches of branching programing. One of them is simple branching or *intrinsic programing*. The intrinsic program 'build' the necessary alternatives into the program itself. Gilman (1972, p. 65) with reference to Crowder (1963), summarise the process of intrinsic programing as follows:

> The student is given a sort description of the material to be learned, following by a multiply- choice question designed to test the point just discussed. The basic intrinsic programing technique, then, amounts to nothing more than the inclusion of multiply-choice questions in relatively conventional expository test and the use of these questions to continually check the students' progress through the material and to finish specific remedial material as it is required.

Unlike Skinner, Crowder's user interfaces includes the frame for communication between user and author through immediate feedback. The linear sequence includes frames with more text for reading and require response to an adjunct question, provided usually is a multiple-option format. The feedback corrective. Thus, if the student makes a correct response, the program asserts the reasons why the response is correct and moves on to new material. However, if the response is incorrect, the program inform the user that an error was made and then branches the user back to the previous frame for another attempt. One version of Crowder's schema is presented in Fig. 2.1.

Differences between Skinner's and Crowder's approach of linear thinking are in Table 2.1.

The model of full branching is *adaptive programming*. Gilman (1972, p. 65) with reference to Crowder (1963) note that adaptive programing is extrinsic, because some external device assists in the control of the program. These programs permit analyse of a student response and the arrangement of the future learning contingent

Fig. 2.1 Crowder's schema to design the branching program

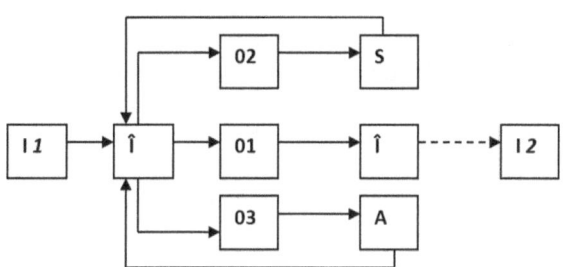

Table 2.1 Skinner's instead of Crowder's approach of linear thinking

	Skinner	Crowder
Content	Small frames	Large frames
Feedback	Positive/negative learning	Corrective learning
Level of abilities	Lower-ability user	Higher-ability user

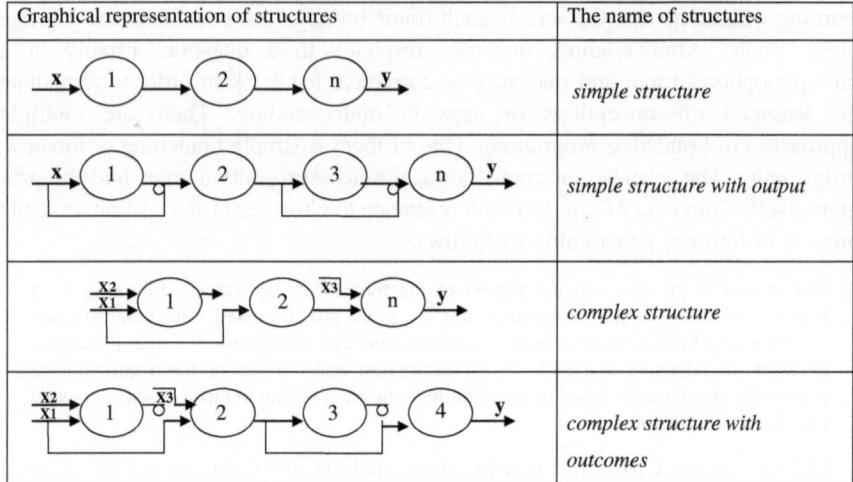

Graphical representation of structures	The name of structures
	simple structure
	simple structure with output
	complex structure
	complex structure with outcomes

Fig. 2.2 The graphical representation of logical—structural scgemas

in the light of students' characteristics and student's response. In our day, when personal computers and Internet have reshaped media, the educational technology is changing also. There are multiple examples of adaptive textbooks with person-alised content, whiteboards and projection screens. One of this way is using of the logical—structural schemas, as it is presented in Fig. 2.2.

Indeed, the technology promises to offer a new way for learning, but until now didn't solve the problem how to engage all students in adaptive learning. As was written in New Scientist (2014), adaptive learning is struggling to provide under-standing of subjects for middle students, while faster learners can surge ahead without getting the bored learning at computer.

Develop the design principles for interactive content. In their opinion, the psy-chological principles involves the nature of memory and mental structures, the nature of conscious and unconscious attention, response time and time to learn, the nature of errors, learning and problem solving strategies, the role of language in cognition, encoding processes and gulfs of understanding. However, the graphic design principles focus on issues of composition: layout, weight, color, positive/negative space and balance; color: color combinations, colored type and the psychology of color; type: typeface, type styles, legibility and the psychology of type; and graphics: graphic elements, color, placement, and integration into an overall design.

2.4 Systems Thinking and Systems Dynamics

Since 1970 schools began acquiring computers and use them for instruction, drill and practice, record keeping and other things. Since 1900 textbooks have migrated to digital and tablets. However, in both cases educational software programs were developed on the base on linear and systems thinking. According to systems thinking approach, the learning, on the bases of instructional system design, follows a well-established algorithmic model. The core model is ADDIE (where A-analyses, D-design, D-development, I-Implementation, and E-evaluation). Therefore, instructional design model based on systems thinking helps designers to make sense of abstract learning theory and enable real applications for instruction and assessment.

Until now, it was developed many instructional systems, including educational software, eBook/iBook, digital textbooks and others. Instead these systems embody the instructional objectives and are developed on the base on ADDIE model, theirs effectiveness for learning is not proved with the empirical research. Moreover, the holistic approach in the systems thinking means to derive understanding of parts from the behavior and proprieties of wholes rather that derive the behavior and proprieties of wholes from those of their parts. When holistic approach is integrated within the ADDIE model, the results are not better. What are the reasons?

First, in rapidly changing paradigms. Second, in the development of new concepts related on systems theory, like feedback, system, learning process, learning objects etc. Thus, the design patterns of the multimedia/interactive/adaptive textbooks come from the systems theory. However, with the extensive application of artificial intelligence and cognitive theory it was developed new tools, like *cognitive tutor*. But, those seeking to understand the meaning and the importance of the cognitive tutor for learning in a diversity of environments, first is confused by a diverse of the terminological terms associated with other terms, e.g. computer-assisted instruction, computer based education, computer based instruction, computer-enriched instruction, computer managed instruction, organisational learning and others.

In the actual textbook theory, 'systems thinking' is connected with thinking in complexity, in which the systems' parts have interrelated and worked over time within the dynamic and flexible context. In brief, all elements are working together to enhance the instructional/learning/assessment processes as well as all students in the learning process. All processes are managed at the level of metasystems. In a certain sense, it can be said that systems thinking is as old as educational philosophy if this is an equivalent to controllable activities and rational actions. In all other cases, when the student learns to grow (as a child, as a specialist, as a professional etc.).

Systems thinking has used in education and, therefore, in user interface design of school textbook before the concept of system was described in the General System Theory (Von Bertalanffy 1972a, b) and it was formalised the notions of feedback (Wiener 1948). For example, the *Orbis* textbook, originally published by Comenius in 1648, includes table of context and content according to a program, including 150 pictures. Such textbook attempts youngs in learning more effectively than grammatical handbooks. Indeed, the pictorial mode within the system thinking 'holds' together table of contents and content. This is the simplest and the most effective model of systems thinking, used until today.

Nevertheless, systems can be closed or/and open. The closed system is an isolated system, not interacting with an environment. The equivalent of the closed system for education is the pedagogical system. Each of the pedagogical systems is an artificial designed system, which provide the abstracted content for learning not related with an environment issues, e.g. sustainable development. Frick (1991) observes that telecommunication technologies make the educational system much more open and flexible and estimates that a variety of "virtual teachers" and educational resources can be used every time and everywhere. Thus, the actual educational system archives new features, which are more or less focused on openness.

But, according to theory an open system changes its behavior in response to conditions outside its boundaries. Therefore, in on open educational system, learning occurs in more complex and changeable learning environments than in all artificially designed pedagogical closed systems. One attempt to understand the complexity of learning, and therefore, the design of real learning environment is the *Bronfenbrenner's Ecological System Theory* (Bronfenbrenner 1994, p. 38), based on two postulates:

- human development takes places through processes of progressively more complex reciprocal interaction between an active, evolving biopsychological human organism and the persons, objects, and symbols in its immediate environment;
- the form, power, content and direction of the proximal processes effecting development vary systematically as a join function of the characteristic of the developing person; of the environment – both immediate and more remote in which the processes are taking places, and the nature of the development outcomes under consideration.

The other attempt is to use the concept of *systems dynamics* (Angerhofer and Angelide 2016) to solve real problems through understanding the nonlinear behavior of complex systems over time using stocks, flows, internal feedback loops, and time delays. However, in reality systems thinkers are more comfortable when can integrate new and old knowledge in a systematic way. They are impatient with step-by-step instructions, but prefer to divide learning blocks into 'bigger steps', to follows instructional objectives and, for understanding, to add formative assessment during each steps (Sadler 1989). At the final stage, they prefer summative assessment or testing. In many cases, systems thinkers require linear thinking methodologies for problem-solving, especially algorithms.

In user interface design of digital textbook the system(s) approach is valued through *Instructional System Design* or *System Design*, defining the process of designing and developing efficient instructional courses or instructional materials to acquiring knowledge or skills. Instructional designers, trained to use a systematic approach to designing new instructional systems or to improving already existing systems, use Instructional System Design approach. Therefore, there are many instructional systems models.

According to Dick et al. (2001, p. 18), the basic components of systematically designed instruction are learning activities packages and modules. Thus,

> A module is usually a self-instructional printed unit of instruction that has an integrated theme, provides students with information needed to acquire and assess specified knowledge and skills, and serves as one component of a total curriculum.<...>. Systematically designed instruction require learner to interact with the instructional material rather than simply allowing them to read the material passively. The learners are asked to perform various types of learning tasks and receive feedback on that performance. Some type of testing strategy informs the learners whether they achieved mastery of the content and what they should do, if not.

The most important elements are language, layout, and design of content. The size, color, and placement of each element 'work together', forming a holistic whole for perception. Instead of printed content, the digital content may include *variables*, like text, audio, and video messages. 'System variables such as interactivity and clear audio and video transmission positively influenced perceived learning and satisfaction' (Hackman and Walker 1990). For this record, the user interfaces of digital textbooks should be appropriate to those *design styles* and *user interfaces* that students prefer. A consistent content with a clear hierarchy enables students to focus on the most important things. Therefore, the good interfaces of digital textbook speak to the student; even his/her actions are right, wrong or misunderstood.

Moreover, visual, audio cues or simple messaging informs show the user whether his or her actions have led to the expected results. In case of the mistakes, the instructional system informs the student by showing what was wrong and how the prevent the error from occurring again. It is important to reward students within teaching situations with positive feedback or, at least, writing in a positive way. All user interfaces require copywriting. The information is provided in conversational form with clear and concise labels for actions. User interfaces require some level of copywriting. Keep things conversational, not sensational. Provide clear and concise labels for actions and keep your messaging simple. Your users will appreciate it, because they won't hear you—they will hear themselves and/or their peers.

While "linear thinking forces use to see one thing at a time, and to progress to whatever is next, which will in turn lead to more" (Risku and Harding 2013), systems thinking for centuries was overlooked. As was noted by Lazanski (2010) systems thinking emphases looking at wholes rather than parts, and addresses the role of interconnections. It is a circular and focused on closed interdependences. It has precise set of rules that reduced the ambiguities and miscommunications that can crop up when we talk with others about complex issues. It offers causal loop diagrams, which are rich in implications and insight. The modern systems thinking principles are:

- the big picture.
- long term, short term perspectives.

- measurable and no measurable data.
- dynamic, complex and interdependent.
- we are a part of system.

In the opinion of Lazanski (2010, pp. 293–295), the systems thinking offer an entirely different ways of communications and of working together more productive on understanding and solving complex problem. Regarding the methodology of systems thinking, the system thinking is usually investigated by questionnaires, video analysis, or interviews and concept-mapping technique. The answer could be yes/true, a number, a word or a sentence. As result, through the user interface design the system will communicate the answer to student or will engage student in a pedagogical dialogue. For example, on display is provided a statement 2 + 2 = □ and the learner will write Is this an example of linear or systems thinking? Could these examples be used for problem-solving skills? Each of the systems works step-by-steps. This means that in case of problem solving the issue can be broken in small steps and the student needs to pass one step in order to perform the next step.

For example, if the student passes step I the current value of his/her input for next step will be Xi and the internal cognitive state will be Si which could be transformed into the output value Yi+1 with state Si+1 and so on, according to the corresponding functions. Is this possible using knowledge management systems, for example Moodle or ATutor? If yes, what is Data Visualization Criteria and how the user interfaces need to be designed?

Is this useful to apply systems theory in user interface design of digital textbook? In time when modelling aims to obtain the core structure of competence during learning with/without digital textbooks the design and development of the students' cognitive and behavioural actions are the main issue of systems thinking. The proposed assumption is that correct or incorrect answers need to be proved by feedback from real environments.

2.5 Metasystems Thinking

The postmodernism theory emphases the impact of metacognition on learning. Let us analyse principles of user interface design starting from the postmodernism philosophy. According to the definition, the postmodernism philosophy is associated with the deconstruction and post-structuralism. In our point of view, metacognition may be modelled on the base on MetaSystems Learning Design. Learning is valid when metacognitive strategies are used effectively. Therefore, discrete parameter stochastic processes, changes in probability of occurrence of a response in a small time is more about requirements for effective learning and not about the effective learning processes through digital textbooks.

That is the big difference between our artificially developed skills to project linearly and real world. It's what's really causing *disruptive behaviour of the best students* because they hardly learn how to solve artificial designed tasks in a linear way, but the world's tasks are more complex and the knowledge is changing exponentially. So a best student that was trained in a linear way doesn't see the exponential digital technology coming out of right field and can put them out of business. Meanwhile, the student who weren't so good in formal schooling may found a company going from zero to billions that are growing in exponential curves.

The modern digital textbook design is assumed to be the coherent product of an author and users of content. The MetaSystems thinking approach involve design and development of the cognitive, affective and psychomotor frameworks. This means that author of the digital textbooks need to think not only about the content, but also about the interfaces, learning styles, how the users will access graphics, assessment tasks etc. Moreover, it is important to estimate the consistencies of screen design, changing colours, font sizes, etc. on different digital devices, as well as to estimate the learning outcomes.

The user interface design needs to be more than an instructional or assessment design.

According to Klir (1990, p. 325), meta X are used as the name of things or systems, which are more than X in sense than it is more organised, have higher logical type of organisation and it is analysed in more general case. Our hypothesis is:

if a digital content contains hypertext or multimodal text, it can be personalised. However, this content should be integrated in a feedback loop with immediate and delayed feedback and will contain a concept mapping tool that will assure a powerful learning environment.

Metasystems approach to learning design relies on post-modernism philosophy of learning, architecture of integrative structure of competence, user interface design principles and learner-centered learning environments. Moreover, conceptual modelling is based on the following principles:

- *principle of self-regulation* (the automatic regulation of learning processes through activation of metacognition using didactical and psychological methods, cybernetics techniques and management systems);
- *principle of personalisation* (the individualization of learning objects through increased formation of the individual as a self and as a member of global learning community);
- *principles of feedback diversity* (electronic educational context needs to be evaluated through immediate and delayed feedback);
- *principle of clarity* (the formation of structural skeleton content with powerful interconnected concepts);
- *principle of dynamism and flexibility* (the learner' active inclusion in elaboration of the content in order to provide the competence development skills)
- *principle of ergonomics* (computer based learning and computer based assessment is guided by ergonomic interfaces and ergonomic places of work).

Analysing the metasystems approach to learning design as educational outcomes of learning, we realised that the evolution of informational technologies conduct to metasystems thinking as an output in learning with electronic textbook. This result is achieved when user interface design criteria provide the evidence of the inter-dependences between information/communication, cognitive and assessment processes.

If so, the students should know not only *cognitive strategies* to complete a variety of academic tasks, but also to effectively apply the *metacognitive strategies*. The metacognitively sophisticated learners invoke both metacognitive strategies (designed to monitor cognitive progress) and cognitive strategies (designed to make cognitive progress). The problem is that some strategies have reliable behavioural indicators, and others do not. However, both readily observed and not readily observed are worthy objects of scientific investigation.

In plus, development of the cognitive and metacognitive strategies requires attentional resources, can be examined, reported and modified by an external 'technological system', and is needed for flexible use. According to Carner (1988, p. 64) the knowing when to use a strategy is as important as knowing how to use it. Therefore, the metacognitively sophisticated learners know whether or not the criterion the criterion task to be completed warrants the costly expenditure of time and effort involved in strategic processing. The values of metacognitive strategies are: creative thinking, critical thinking, design thinking (ecological/sustainable/regenerative design), flexible thinking, futures thinking/anticipatory thinking, flexible thinking, lateral thinking, reflective thinking, and strategic thinking.

References

Angerhofer, B. J., & Angelides, M. C. (2000). *System dynamics modelling in supply chain management: research review. In Proceedings of Simulation Conference, 2000,* Winter (Vol. 1, pp. 342–351). IEEE.

B. F. Skinner's Theory. http://www.theoryfundamentals.com/skinner.htm

Benjamin, L. T. (1988). A history of teaching machines. *American Psychologist, 43*(9), 703–712.

Bosch, O., & Nguyen, N. (2016). Capacity Building and Think2Impact. In *Proceedings of the 59th Annual Meeting of the ISSS-2015 Berlin, Germany* (Vol. 1, No. 1).

Bronfenbrenner, U. (1994). Ecological Models of Human Development. http://www.psy.cmu.edu/~siegler/35bronfebrenner94.pdf

Crowder, N. A. (1963). On the differences between linear and intrinsic programing. *The Phi Delta Kappan, 44*(6), 250–254.

Dick, W., Carey, L., & Carey, J. O. (2001). *The systematic design of instruction.* New York: Longman.

Eigen, L. D. (1962). A comparison of three modes of presenting a programmed instruction sequence. *The Journal of Educational Research, 55*(9), 453–460.

Flynn, N. (2016). Performativity and Metaphor in New Materialist Media theory. *networking knowledge. Journal of the MeCCSA Postgraduate Network, 9*(1).

Frick, T. W. (1991). Restructuring Education through Technology. Phi Delta Kappa Educational Foundation. Bloomington: Indiana. https://www.indiana.edu/~tedfrick/fastback/fastback326. html/. Accessed 05.04.16

Gilman, D. A. (1972). The origins and development of intrinsic and adaptive programing. *Educational Technology Research and Development, 20*(1), 64–76.

Ha, T. M., Bosch, O. J., & Nguyen, N. C. (2016). Practical Value of the systems-based evolutionary learning laboratory in solving complex community problems in Vietnam. In *Proceedings of the 59th Annual Meeting of the ISSS-2015 Berlin, Germany* (Vol. 1, No. 1).

Hackman, M. Z., & Walker, K. B. (1990). Instructional communication in the televised classroom: The effects of system design and teacher immediacy on student learning and satisfaction. *Communication Education, 39*(3), 196–206.

Hairston, M. (1982). The winds of change: Thomas Kuhn and the revolution in the teaching of writing. *College composition and communication, 33*(1): 76–88. http://www.reiffad.com/genre/Hairston.pdf

Handani, M., Charbaghi, A., & Sharifuddin, R. S. (2011). Instructional design approaches, types and trends. A foundation for postmodernism instructional design. *Australian Journal of Basic and Applied Sciences, 5*(8), 1–7.

Hjorth, P., & Bagheri, A. (2006). Navigating towards sustainable development: A system dynamics approach. *Futures, 38*(1), 74–92.

INNEPS. (2016). Productive learning. What is it? http://www.ineps.org/pdf/Productive%20Learning.pdf

Joyce, B., Weil, M., & Calhoun, E. (2000). Models of teaching, 6th edn. Allyn & Bacon.

Karsvall, A. (2002). Personality preferences in graphical interface design. *In Proceedings of the second Nordic conference on Human-computer interaction* (pp. 217–218). ACM.

Klir, G. (1990). *Architecture of systems problem solving*. New York and Longon: Plenum Press. (In Russian).

Lazanski, T. J. (2010). Systems thinking: ancient Maya's evolution of consciousness and contemporary systems thinking. *AIP Conference Proceedings, 1303*(1), 289–296.

Liu, Y., Wu, M., & Sun, Z. (2014). Extending the TAM model to explore the factors that affect intention to use digital textbooks in primary teachers' views. *Intelligent Environments*. Workshop Proceeding of 10th International Conference on Intelligent Environments, 127–136.

Merrill. D. First Principles of Instruction. http://mdavidmerrill.com/Papers/firstprinciplesbymerrill.pdf

Montuori, A. (2012). *Reproductive learning. In Encyclopedia of the Sciences of Learning* (pp. 2838–2840). Springer, US.

New scientist (2014). Digital textbooks adapt to your level as you learn. https://www.newscientist.com/article/mg22329832-600-digital-textbooks-adapt-to-your-level-as-you-learn/

Richmon, B. (1994) System Dynamics/Systems Thinking: Let's Just Get On With It, International Systems Dynamics Conference, Sterling, Scotland http://www.iseesystems.com/resources/Articles/SDSTletsjustgetonwithit.pdf

Risku, M., Harding, L. (2013). A unified theory. In: M. Risku & L. Harding (Eds.), *Education for tomorrow: A Biocen A Biocentric, student-focused model for reconstructing education* (pp. 113–134). SensePublishers.

Sadler, D. R. (1989). Formative assessment and the design of instructional systems. *Instructional science, 18*(2), 119–144, http://pdf.truni.sk/e-ucebnice/iktv/data/media/iktvv/Symposium_LTML_Royce%20Sadler_BFormative_Assessment_and_the_design_of_instructional_systems.pdf

Schlesinger, P., & Waelde, C. (2011). Performers on the edge [video]. *Audiovisual thinking, 2011* (3).

Skinner, B. F. (1965). Reflection on a decade of teaching machines. Perspectives and Technology. Teaching machine and programed learning. In Glaser, R (Ed.), *ERIC: National Education Association*, Washington, D.C.

Smith, K. U., & Smith, M. F. (1966). Cybernetic principles of learning and educational design. Holt, Rinehart and Winston.

Tchulkina, N. L., & Garbar, O. V. (2016). Secondary Linguocultural Consciousness in the "Instaworld": Modern Teenager's World Outlook Forming by Means of the "Picture Creative Thinking" Technology. *Mediterranean Journal of Social Sciences, 7*(1), 449–459.

Teal, R. (2010). Developing a (non-linear) practice of design thinking. *International Journal of Art & Design Education.*, *29*(3), 294–302.

Universal Design of Learning. http://www.cast.org/our-work/about-udl.html#.V2ZSnqKPVKA

Viegas, F., Wattenberg, M. (2011), How To Make Data Look Sexy. http://articles.cnn.com/2011-04-19/opinion/sexy.data_1_visualization-21st-century-engagement?_s=PM:OPINION

Visser, W. (2006). The cognitive artifacts of designing. Lawrence Erlbaum Associates.

Von Bertalanffy, L. (1972a). The history and status of general systems theory. *Academy of Management Journal, 15*(4), 407–426.

Von Bertalanffy, L. (1972b). The meaning of general system theory. General system theory: Foundations, development, applications, 30–53.

Wiener, N. (1948). *Cybernetics: Or control and communication in the animal and the machine.* Paris, Cambridge & Massachusetts: Hermann & Cie, MIT Press.

Chapter 3
Digital Screens and Issues of Multiliteracies' Learning

> *I cannot teach anybody anything,*
> *I can only make them think.*
>
> Socrates

Abstract Digital screen is the main pattern of the digital revolution. Around the world schools and universities, changes printed pages in favour of digital screens, creating innovative platforms for learning and assessment methodologies, however many others keep the traditional approaches of teaching and printed textbooks. The new paradigm of learning is focused on development the vital competence for sustainability. Although educational system has been opened by the globalisation, the diversity of digital screens is a big challenge for this process. How digital affects the opening process of the educational system and, therefore, changes the behaviour? This scientific question inspired the ideas presented in this chapter. The aim of this chapter is to compare the features of digital screen with the intention of multiliteracies' learning.

Keywords Digital screen · Digital natives · Behaviour · Multiliteracies

3.1 Introduction

Openness, nano-learning and networking of the pedagogical systems form the conceptual framework of the modern education. Books, textbooks, television, radio and classrooms are 'converging' into new patterns for learning. The foregoing scenario is only for a short period because of rapidly changing paradigms. The question it raises it 'Will the actual students of law, medicine and economics in ten years' time be equipped to enhance the contribution of the profession in the circumstances described above?'. To make a judgement of this, it is necessary to consider not only technological, but also the philosophical, psychological, pedagogical and other paradigms that command the complex process.

Digital screens has used to display and shared data for the most effective dissemination of information. In reality, we see many students using digital for gaming or social media. They don't want to read or to learn something new. If it is expected that digital textbooks is a tool enabling to engage students for active participation in the learning process, we should understand that students should be motivated enough for this.

According to finding of MacArthur Foundation project, the way in which young people learn, play, socialize, and participated in civic life is changing considerable. However, there are *direct* and *indirect* impacts on learning. On one hand, using digital media allows freedom and authonomy or youth that is less apparent in a classroom setting (e.g. direct impact). On the other hand, digital communication have altered: picking up the basic and technological skills in curriculum and/or extra-curriculum activities; increasing various kinds of social connotations within friendship-driven and interest-driven online participation; and learning from peers and not from teachers and adults, which framed negatively development of behavior.

Youths' participation in networked world suggests new ways of thinking about user interface design (e.g. indirect impact). Furthermore, digital screens can be an ideal place for collaborative assessment, as a context for learning. The problem is that printed textbooks cannot be used within social media and education 3.0 paradigm. The paradigm changes the way in theory and practice of design thinking and, therefore, should propose a new learning theory.

Education 3.0 is a connectionist and heutagogical approach of user-generated content. Digital content of the textbooks are displayed as: (a) *text*—scrolling text—interactive text—adaptive text etc.; (b) *images*—scrolling images—interactive images—adaptive images; (c) videos—interactive videos—adaptive streaming—3D film; or a (d) *multimodal* text, which combines two or more semiotic systems, like linguistic, visual, audio, gestural and spatial. Moreover, instead of printed text that allow only one communication, digital textbooks allow two-way communication (e.g. hypertext) or three-way communication (e.g. hermeneutic dialogue) with the users In all cases the content of the digital textbooks should be *responsive*.

The term 'literacy' defines the ability to read, to write and to use arithmetic (Barton 2007). More recently this term appears to be a synonym of tangible skills for writing, reading, oral communication and calculus. Cope and Kalantzis (2000, p. 9) consider that literacy pedagogy is restricted to formalised, monolingual, monocultural and rule governed forms of language and that it is important to have a broaden understanding of this term, taking into account not only the content, but also the context for learning. Thus, pedagogy must account for the burgeoning variety of text forms associated with information and multimedia technologies.

3.2 Multiliteracies and Online Textbooks, Systems, Platforms, Screens, Channels, and Apps

The term 'multiliteracies' is used to focus pedagogy on finding adequate solutions for the problems of linguistic diversity, and multimodal forms of linguistic expression and representation. However, although academic institutions are developed the technological infrastructure and support this investment, in fact, these investments are not related only on multiliteracies. The most of the students are using special languages, both for reading and writing, 'developed' in virtual environment. These languages are more attractive for them; although in schools are thousands of lessons every year. What is the reason?

There are many reasons, but one of the most important is that education is more focused on direct or systemic consequences of instruction and assessment that on identification the issues and developing the adequate solutions. The grammar is no longer needed for students and the cognitive filters are blocked all information regarding the rules? Or, maybe the strategy or methods used by teachers is so old, that students are trying to find other, more innovative way for learning like self-regulated learning, as was observed by De Corte (2016). Maybe, from this reason they are looking for some other textbooks, those content is more compact, have a higher level of organization and is presented in a more logical way.

On the other hand, technology has proposed various knowledge management systems, platforms, screens, apps and other innovations that are more attractive than the bored lessons in schools and universities. However, if the knowledge management systems are mainly used by teachers to disseminate the content in a virtual environment. Both teacher and students use all others because it is more available, visually attractive, and in some cases, it is easier. In plus, same teachers use platforms to develop own textbooks, e.g. Khan Academy, Ridero etc.

Developing own textbooks on the base on available on-line platforms is a global phenomenon. As was noted by Blaschke (2012), education proposed a special form of self-determined learning 'heutagogy', with practices and principles rooted in andragogy, learners are highly autonomous and self-determined and emphasis is placed on development of learner capacity and capability with the goal of producing learners who are well-prepared for the complexities of today's workplace. A key concept is heutagogy is of double loop learning and self-reflection. In double loop learning, the learner consider the problem and the resulting action and outcomes, in addition to reflecting out the problem-solving process and how it influences the learner own beliefs and actions. Heutagogy is a bridge between self-directed and self-regulated learning. However, if the traditional pedagogical model is 'teacher→learner directed', the heutagogical model is learner directed. However, the capacity to self-direct learning is not genetic and, therefore, getting students to know how to learn is not enough. First, they need to be engaged in a powerful learning environment in order to motivate and, second, they need to keep this motivation for learning. Third, it is very important to develop such 'structure' of competence that will keep the motivation for all life (e.g. life-long learning).

Education textbook market is stuck between several countervailing trends. On one hand, the professors and their students are still use printed textbooks as the core reading resource, but also interactive whiteboard for teaching and assessment. At the same time, they use digital and digitalized textbooks for self-directed learning. Moreover, some of professors customize the digital content according to students' needs or learning styles. In addition, teachers and students have much more ways to get the needed content via digital libraries, repositories or/and open source textbooks, that were not available a decade ago.

Dispute the widespread assumption that digital media are changing the ways in how student's brains are learning in various learning environments, screen, channels; there is a hot area of research related on changing behavior that indicate toward a new pedagogy for multiliteracies (The New London Group 1996; Luke 2000; Cope and Kalantzis 2000, 2009; Selber 2004; Anstey and Bull 2006). Rapid evolution of the digital revolution require changing the terms 'literacy' and 'literacy pedagogy' taking into account that the term 'multiliteracies' defining skills to gain knowledge through technology, as well as the capacity of the lifelong learners to learn for well-being in a digital society.

As was noted by Cope and Kalantzis (2000, p. 19) the metalanguage of the multiliteracies is based on the concept of 'Design', meaning that teachers and managers are seen as designers of the learning processes and environments. This means that the pedagogy should interrelate with the domain of design science, taking into account the differences between cultural, pedagogical and classroom designs models and patterns. Therefore, the increasing multiplicity and the integration of the various models of meaning for lifelong learners indicate that students' patterns for learning already have integrated in a holistic whole the visual, the audio, the spatial, and the behavioural patterns.

Anderson (2011) notes that digital displays are essential tools for supporting students learning and making the classroom feel welcoming and engaging. The best way to archive these results is to include everyone in a *digital learning environment*, in which interactive whiteboard and digital textbooks form a holistic whole. For this, digital screen allows displaying work from every children as well as drafts and finishing work side by side, giving students a say about what you highlights makes displays more interesting to them, reinforces their efforts, and fosters a feeling of community as they see that the classroom is something they create together. Moreover, putting pieces at the student's eye level. It is very important to choose the right space, to control clutter and to keep displays fresh. Therefore, overdoing displays, even those of students' work, can overstimulate children and interfere with your efforts to create a calm classroom environment.

Today, in many countries of the world, leaders have discussed the challenges of making the transition from paper to digital in very short time. Digital means, among others, using of the *digital devices* in all schools and universities. Instead of the learning with printed textbooks, that is only an object for reading; a digital textbook on digital device has the potential to establish a *digital learning environment,* which may be an indicator of active learning in an environment with interactive whiteboard, educational software, digital textbooks and *active learners*. The active learners are those that are able to initiate, to plan, to implement, to control, to evaluate and to apply their learning themselves. For this, as was noted by Peters (2000), not only factual knowledge is important, but also competence in using the methods of obtaining it as well as competence of co-operating with others. Therefore, in a digital learning environment, several presentation methods can be combined and integrated; multi-sensory instruction can be strengthened; interactivity can be extended quantitatively and qualitatively and support system can be extended and improved.

Moreover, in a digital learning environment is used many digital objects for learning. However, when a physical unit of equipment (e.g. a device or a whiteboard) has integrated with an educational software the teacher/learner has more than a physical object for learning. Indeed, such a unit has a *digital screen,* which is a special area on which media, images, text and data has displayed. Different screens have various sizes, features, and functionalities. In the most of cases, the user, even teacher or student, can easy manipulate the items by using his/her finger or a mouse directly on the screen for dragged, clicked, copied, deleted and sent through Internet. Thus, digital screens have used for interactive activities, and some—only for reading. How affordance of the digital screen affects learning?

The content of the digital screen is stored in various forms: PDF, HTML, and others. The problem of how these formats for active learning can be used in digital learning environment is now of considerable *pedagogical* importance. There are many possibilities. However, if on digital screen of students' devices is uploaded the PDF version of the printed textbooks, but on interactive whiteboard—presentation of concepts in an interactive, adaptive or flexible manner, during lesson the teacher will have the priority of interactive whiteboard.

Ideally, the digital features of the interactive whiteboard screen has repeated on students' displays. One of these features is *Apps,* which allows adding annotations, highlighting text, adding notes and drawing, labelling parts or highlighting elements of an image in a teacher-directed activity, even in learning with pdf versions of the digital textbooks. What effect do interactive features has on students' brains? For example, if it is used the tandem of Mobi View™ and students' tablets, a functional large LCD touch screen has the priority because allow teachers to control the lesson from everywhere in the classroom. On the other hand, with an effective method this tandem motivates students not only to absorb information, but also to create new knowledge at the level of understanding.

The other example has presented by Cinganotto et al. (2016, pp. 117–120). TEAL (e.g. Technology Enabled Active Learning), as an innovative teaching model to address several of educational problems: (a) in a lecture based courses in which lectures 'delivered' content with additional smaller recitation sections, the failure rates were high, as result of very low retention rates of core physical concepts, working in teams and developing communicative skills. This competence is needed to be developed in a more adaptive and flexible instructional environment. Therefore, the TEAL methodology employs the interactive group structure, as well as two and three-dimensional visualisation, animations and simulations that allow students to explore and understand better the phenomenon, reactions and events. The best teaching/learning strategies in a TEAL environment are problem posing/solving to develop critical thinking skills; cooperative learning and discovery learning in small groups or in pairs; peer tutoring and peer learning and learning by hand-on experiments to develop active involvement in the learning process. Moreover, TEAL methodology refers on inductive methods from the observation and the practice to the conceptual frame; concept questions with individual reflection, peer discussion, corrective feedback from the teacher; challenges based learning, launching challenges to the students through a gamification process; project based learning working with the aim to produce a project through artefacts (e.g. video, tutorials etc.). In plus, there are very important to use experimentations, visualisations, simulations, task-based learning activities according to specific tasks and interactive presentations and Open Educational Resources.

Furthermore, in an university learning environment may be used *learning analytics*. As was written in Educause, with reference to *2016 Horizon Report the learning analytics* is an educational application of web analytics aimed at learner profiling, a process of gathering and analysing details of individual student interactions in online learning activities. Following the review of the scientific literature, it has to say that the learning analytics reveal patterns aims to improve learning for individual students as well as across institutions, predicting what will happen in the future and what methods is better to develop competence for future jobs.

In a digital society, learning is a part of the metasystems functionality for sustainability. In such a conceptualisation, the learner cannot be more view only as an empirical observer and experimenter, as was defined by Locke, or as a reader of the pictorial textbooks, as was identified by Comenius. Learner, today, has new aims, strategies, visions, and knows how and where is better for him to learn to be agile, adaptive and inventive. However, a diversity of digital screens, from interactive whiteboards to smartphones, used in formal and informal learning environments are giving rise to a new pedagogy of learning.

Nevertheless, what is the subject line of new pedagogy? It is a widely accepted that education is a key driving force for *sustainable development* of the world. Noguchi et al. (2015, p. 12) observe the emergence of the field called Education for Sustainable Development (ESD), characterised by active participation of the people in the development of a world for everyone and for social transformation of activities, knowledge, skills and values related on how learning takes place and how should be in the future.

As the digital revolution has increased the number of bits and challenges in education, many pedagogical questions aroused, also. Learning from a personal acquisition of knowledge in one domain to has transformed toward lifelong competency. Therefore, on one hand, the lifelong learning is important for sustainable learning environment and on other hand, the lifelong learning needs new (meta) cognitive self-development strategies.

3.3   The Main Features of a Learning Society

The term "learning society", coined by Hutchins (1969), refers on part-time education available to everyone throughout his life. Today UNESCO that positions education in the centre of formal, non-formal and informal movements toward a learning society quote this term. Building a learning society encompasses learning at all ages and in all possible formats. The proposed by UNESCO strategy 'Building a Learning Strategy' is driven by the principles of lifelong learning. Computers and digital devices are the fact of life in a learning society.

Textbooks with the previously established instructional objectives will continue to deplete in favour of digital textbooks. The learning society is a part of the sustainable world that face digital textbooks to provide the self-regulated potential in the next future. As was noted by Scheunpflug et al. (2016, p. 6) the global learning aims to change behaviour and attitudes toward learning for sustainability. Thus, first, encourages dialogue among businesses and organisation of the need to create living organizations in harmony with the natural and social world. In a sustainable world, human and natural systems can thrive together. In spite of these notes, provided by Laur et al. (2006, p. 3) many of the basic assumptions of pedagogy are scientific questions: What kind of information for students should be presented? How to transform information in sustainable knowledge and skills? What is the impact of technology on educational outcomes?

Now, we are living in the complexity of environments, challenges, technologies. Updating pedagogy for a sustainable development is the main condition in a learning society. How to ensure this condition? In practice, the design of learning environment remains only an individual or/and collaborative activity, which is a teacher-cantered or learner-cantered. Such conceptualisation cannot guarantee development of competency for a sustainable world.

Let us analyse the diversity of learning environments available in the last years. With the comparative methods could be easy observe that the thirty-two most innovative online educational tools to use in 2015 can be classified, as follows (Fig. 3.1):

Fig. 3.1 Eight categories of tools for learning

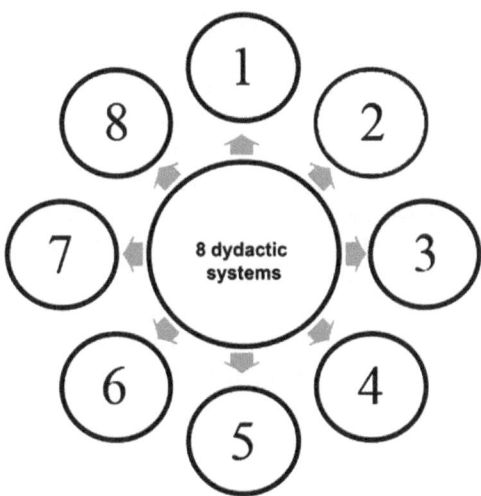

The categories of online innovative educational tools are:

1. *Classroom connections*—students, teachers and parents are login into all tools with a single set of credentials and do same activities (e.g. Clever, Edmodo, Kahoot!; Schoology, Skype etc.);
2. *Interactive Information Providers*—teacher(s) and students are get information that are better explained through videos, diagrams, explanations, sketches (e.g. BetterExplained; Desmos, etc.);
3. *Knowledge Graph*—teacher(s) and/with students are find information (e.g. text, videos, free video tutorials) in order to understand the meaning and for assignment through Voice Search, Carousel, instaGrok, Khan Academy; PatrickJMT, Wolfram Alpha;
4. *Language Learning Tools*—an intuitive, step-by-step learning progression that leads speakers through the basics of the language while gently challenging them and explaining key grammatical concepts like Duolingo, Pleco, SpanishDict and others;
5. *Online courses*—free access to free online courses of the best universities through digital platforms, like Coursera and Crash Course or free access to custom-design courses with assignments, materials, and study notes like iTunes U;
6. *Presentation Makers*—creation and sharing graphs through Plotly, make interactive presentation through Prezi; user-created flashcards like StudyBlue; creation of study materials like Quizlet;
7. *Productivity Boosters*—stay focused on same information or task with Cold Turkey; helps create an environment conducive to sleeping with f.lux; analyse the productivity of work on computer through RescueTime; enable to provide help like a friend or a family member with Unstuck;
8. *Reading and Writing Enhancers*—educational reading tools like LightSail, read free audio books with *Books should be free*; free online speed reading with Speeder; write poetry and other creative forms with Poetry Idea Engine and others.

The learning society in the digital age has characterized by the number of data and metadata, language and metalanguage skills, memory and metamemory features, cognition and metacognition skills as well as the ability to apply relevant competence for solving real tasks. In all these cases may be used various tools, resource, including digital textbooks. Therefore, if the content of the digital textbooks is open, the learners' minds have connected with the global learning rules, values and ethics. In a learning society, the content is flexible, interactive, and adaptive. The global environment is rich in (meta)cognitive activities and actions.

Across the globe, can be seen progresses in expanding open access for reading textbooks. However, the aspiration of students for comprehensive digital reading in an open environment requires to solving current-future pedagogical issues related on interdependencies between context, content, teacher and students. While development of textbooks contributes to greater interconnectedness between teacher, student, content and context for learning, pedagogy must find non-standard ways of responding to such challenges, taking into account advances in contemporary science.

In a learning society is very important to find a new methodology of *teacher training*. As was noted by Lyashenko (2016, p. 244) the role of a teacher is more complicated because he/she takes not only the role to teach, but also the responsibility to create, to develop, to incorporate, to coordinate, to consult, and to share expertise with the learners. This means that teaching nowadays would require understanding of philosophical trends, students' characteristics, textbooks innovative features as well as the competence 'to combine' new technologies with the traditional ones. Therefore, pedagogy alone cannot solve all global challenges and provide updated solutions for sustainability.

Nevertheless, the learning society is moving toward a digital society (Hayes et al. 2016). The digital society is a progressive society that adopt the concept of sustainable development for living in a 'global village', composed by digital citizen thinking globally, but acting locally. These citizens have the capacity to learn how to access information through an online gateway that works 24/7, and boast the highly advanced telecommunications and wireless connectivity systems and solutions for living. Therefore, citizen of digital society are wellbeing because are adaptive on all challenges.

Digital citizen should have new and more affordable competence. What effect do digital text have on students' brains? Since at least the 2000s researchers in many different fields, including education, psychology, mathetics, and library and information science, and others have investigated this question in more than one hundred published studies (Cull 2011; Jabr 2013; Wollscheid et al. 2016). Thus, all published studies evidence the issue of the *exhaustive reading,* pointing that people understand what they read on printed-paper more thoroughly than what they read on screens.

Now, it is a well-known fact that the brain responds differently to onscreen text than to words on paper. Thus, reading is not a natural act and online digital text represents a revolution in human learning and communication that we are only beginning to understand. Students prefer to get textbook in a digital form, but to print them or, at least, some pages, to read. What is the reason? Definitely, digital technology changes the way of reading/writing the content. As was pointed by Jabr (2013), people are not born with brain circuits dedicated to reading. While an open paperback presents a reader with the left and right pages, and everybody can see where the textbook begins and ends, feeling the thickness of the pages read is in relation to that border, meaning has anchored to whole structure of the textbook. In contrast, digital reading allows searching meaning through highlighting and questioning, which is very different comparative with the printed version.

In addition, digital screen supports children's understanding more effectively, if the teacher direct the pupil's attention to specific points that have to be listening or/and watching, to specific parts of the spoken text or image and/or to develop activities that support understanding. The role of the digital screen is 'to make' as much as possible the effective connections between theory (e.g. scientific concepts from textbooks) and practice for deepen understanding through searching patterns in the real world. One of this connections may be the production of transformed texts, a challenge that, according to Lenters (2016, p. 1) prove the practice to move away from literacy by design and toward literacy as emergence.

Indeed, everywhere it is expected a digital revolution with profound technological, societal, behavioural and even neurological facets. As was noted by Cull (2011) with reference on cognitive neuroscientist Maryanne Wolf (2008) it is expected a shift from the *reading* brain, which has been a hallmark of the human species for millennia, to the *digital brain*. Thus, the digital brain, while reading or writing a digital content, tries to minimalize the required cognitive efforts of multitasking, paratextual elements, and deep sustainable thought and, maybe, the culture of reading and writing. In order to do this it was used different 'technologies', the most important of them was changing the students' behavior.

3.4   Regarding the Issue of Outcomes in a Learning Society

Digital television, social media, social networking, knowledge sharing, online games, video-shared sites and using of various gadgets for messaging are now fixtures of youth. They have so much permeated the human lives, which it is hard to believe that digital technologies barely appears only six decades ago. The actual generation of students, who are born between 1980 and 1994 and claimed to be innovative and prone to changes, is 'Generation Y, Nexters, Echo Boomers, Net Generation and Generation Me' (Majid et al. 2016, p. 685). This generation doing so amid activities for digital networking that want to learn only with technology and Internet. What is the impact of textbooks on learning?

The availability of the digital devises technologies and Internet allows global news changing the ways in which students think and process information, making difficult to excel academically tasks and outdated teaching/assessment methodologies. Who are the students? Tapscott (1998) has observed that most of children of 0–20 years can be called "Net Generation", because they are extremely curious, self-relevant, contrarian, smart, focused, able to adapt, high in self-esteem, and have a global orientation. Students who grow up in a high-tech age and global economy will face a more complex world. For the "Net Generation" working and communicating in an interactive learning environment, both local and global is the best way to explore his/her potential in the world. Therefore, in an interactive learning environments students receive real feedback, which allow competence development.

Prensky (2000) wrote that these are *digital natives*, arguing that actual students have been interacting with digital devices from a very early age, raised in a digital world, gaming in a virtual environment and, the most important they do not like to read. For Howe and Strauss (2000) actual students is *millennials* who need a different type of educational experience. They are more numerous, more social educated, more ethnically diverse; but the most important fact is that, as a group they have an enormous potential power. This generation likes to use digital devices for networking and to be mobile. They do not want to listen the teacher's speech repeatedly about scientific concepts, but intend to understand how theories work in reality.

Ramakrishna (2016) notes that *Net generation* students want to be unicorn in entrepreneurship, innovation and sustainability; they seeks personal fulfilment instead of mere job to care family; they are interested in travel and experience and they are plugged into global digital brain. In plus, Net generation students aspire to develop communication skills, multi-cultural skills, ethnic and social responsibility, interdisciplinary skills. This means, in our point of view, that for the "Net Generation" the printed content of classical textbooks soon will be obsolete. To avoid the failure of the learning in formal schooling, it is already proposed new ways, like a new format of courses: 'each course is broken into short segments of ~11 min that stretch over seven weeks online learning' (Philanthropy University) and digital platforms for global collaborations among different students around a single idea.

However, there are many research regarding psychological learning characteristics of the contemporary students. In order to thrive in/for the sustainable world, students need to understand how to work both individually with own IQ and collaboratively with collective intelligence. As was noted on ISTE (2016), solutions require tenacity, creativity, and critical thinking. While students need to possess core knowledge and skills, they must be adroit with technology and prepared for the demands of the Innovation Age.

How about user interface design of digital textbooks? According to Oviatt (2016, p. 19), computer input capabilities, like a keyboard or pen, substantially influence basic cognitive abilities, including the ability to produce appropriate ideas, solve problems correctly, and make accurate interfaces about information. If it is used for developing representations, modalities, and linguistic codes, this can stimulate human though and performance. This and other facts indicate that instructional designers should be focused not on how to use scanned or digitalised content for learning, but also how to develop critical thinking for sustainable development both of students and of environment, where they live. Thus, drill and practice or multimedia programs are long and bored for the actual students instead of, for example, voice-controlled technology.

There are plenty of ways to incorporate technology into teaching, learning and assessment of actual students. One of this is 'instructional scaffolding', designed to promote a deeper learning, when 'the learning process is tailored to the needs of the student with the intention of helping the student achieve his/her learning goals' (Sawyer 2006). For the instructional scaffolding is important to bring students in an ergonomic digital learning environment; to explain students ergonomics norms; to help students develop specific strategies for listening and/watching information on digital screen; to set specific listening and/watching tasks, emplacing key words; to limit the time for teacher talk, excluding repeating and paraphrasing the student's words.

Today's students have unlimited access to data, information and knowledge. They already live in a highly technological world and to a sustainable development, they should have the generative form of own competence, including relevant knowledge, as well as *skills* to observe, to plan and to prioritize etc. and *attitudes* expressed in capacity to communicate and to network for sustainable development. Thus, thinking and wisdom, in the Prensky's words, is a symbiosis of the human brain, challenges and environment.

One more issue has important on this way should be understood. Since digital textbooks are globally and/or locally developed, the *learning object* for understanding is more important than even. Conversely, when the students have freedom to use open textbooks, this may cause a controversy in provided content and availability of content for learning. The chapter will summarise the impact of digital revolution on literacy through analysing the features of learning society, differences between open educational systems and closed pedagogical systems, terminology of digital textbooks and the issues related no correlation between the digitalisation of didactic triangle and the new meaning of literacy.

3.5 Reflecting on User Interface Design, Learning and ADD/ADHD

Many of the actual students have diagnosed with Attention Deficit Disorder (ADD) and Attention Deficit Hyperactivity Disorder (ADHD). 'Attention-deficit/ hyperactivity disorder (ADHD) or hyperkinetic disorder (HKD) is a common neurodevelopment disorder characterized by developmentally inappropriate levels of inattentive and/or hyperactive-impulsive symptoms that are manifested in multiple setting. <...>. ADHD is associated with impairment in social, academic, and occupational functioning, leading to adverse consequences for affecting individuals, their family and society at large' (Chen 2016). The problem is that the number of children diagnosed with ADD and ADHD are staggering and continue to increase. However, according to Nexus magazine, there are not organic or physiological findings to substantiate the existence of any 'diseases'. Children have diagnosed with ADD when he/she stand when told to sit, fidgeting, and not being happy about doing chores or homework.

The most replicated factors point to define ADD/ADHD are deficits in working memory, response inhibition, vigilance and, planning as well ad time variability, language and speech, and motor control. The full range of ADD/ADHD symptoms may be influences by genetic factors and non-genetic factors. There are no confirmation regarding the correlation between using digital screen for learning and ADD/ADHD symptoms. However, in some cases ADD/ADHD has been associated with overweight and obesity because these children tend to spend more time in watching screen and less time in physical activities.

To avoid increasing ADD/ADHD issues children are treated with stimulant drugs. Pharmacotherapy remains a cornerstone of complex treatment. The most used are Ritalin (methylphenidata and dexamphetamine). But, stimulant drugs pose a long-term risk, could affect the processes of growth and development of child as a social individuum and, the most important thing, may led to depression or other serious diseases. Thus, even these children become more docile and get into 'less trouble', they are not stimulated to learn how to learn. For pedagogy, the scientific knowledge of ADD/ADHD treatment can be view as a body of a complex hypothesis that will lead to a new design approach for learning process.

Indeed, the attention disorder is a big issue of education in a Digital World. In the Ph.D. thesis, Chen (2016) wrote that ADHD is a highly prevalent and clinically heterogeneous neurodevelopment disorder affecting approximatively 3.4–7.3 % children and adolescents and 2.5–3.4 % adults worldwide. It was emphasis the needs to investigate the impact of generic and environmental factors that may lead to these disorders.

Montagni et al. investigated the association of screen time and ADHD. These authors prove well-known facts that students spend increasingly more time watching a screen on TV or on digital devices, including surfing the Internet. Excessive exposure to screen time is associated with unfavourable and unhealthy lifestyle habits, firstly because of low levels of physical activity. However, as for mental health, pathologically excessive screen time exposure may lead to substantial consequences, like a risk marker for anxiety, depression, suicide ideation, which can result in *addictive behaviour*. In plus, increasing levels of screen time exposure is associated with risk of self-perceived attention problems and hyperactivity levels.

In turn, many of the actual students have issues related with the span attention, memory and thinking (Visser 2014; Koenig et al. 2016). Visser (2014) has indicated toward a *temporal attention span*, as the ability to rapidly and accurately process sequences of consecutive target items, which may be limited. Koenig et al. 2016) noted that *selective visual attention* is the property of visual systems to elicit a behavior while at the same **time** equally salient stimuli in other parts do not with a visual stimulus at a particular location of the visual field. These and other studies have indicated *to the issue of investigation the conditions of the learning environments in which students will better focus the visual attention for learning, in particular involving the attention span.*

The memory span and the thinking span is other two issues related on how actual students learn. These issues must be investigated from the interdisciplinary points of view, to understand the real problems of learning actual students and to help them for better educational outcomes. The research questions are: (1) What are the interdependencies between user interface design and educational outcomes? (2) What techniques, methods or strategies are better to span attention, memory and thinking?

References

Anderson, M. (2011). *ASCD Express, 6*(13). http://www.ascd.org/ascd-express/vol6/613-anderson.aspx

Anstey, M., & Bull, G. (2006). *Teaching and learning multiliteracies: Changing times, changing literacies.* International Reading Association. 800 Barksdale Road, PO Box 8139, Newark, DE 19714-8139.

Barton, D. (2007). *Literacy: An introduction to the ecology of written language* (2nd ed.). Wiley-Blackwell.

Blaschke, L. M. (2012). Heutagogy and lifelong learning: A review of heutagogical practice and self-determined learning. http://www.irrodl.org/index.php/irrodl/article/view/1076/2113

Chen, Q. (2016). What can genetically informative designs add to the understanding of ADHD? https://openarchive.ki.se/xmlui/bitstream/handle/10616/45027/Thesis_Qi_Chen.pdf?sequence=1&isAllowed=y/. Accessed April 14, 2016.

Cinganotto, L., Panzavolta, S., Garista, P., Guasti, L., & Dourmashkin, P. (2016). TEAL as an innovative teaching model Insights from "Educational Avant-Garde" Movement in Italy. *Journal of e-Learning and Teaching Society.* http://www.je-lks.org/ojs/index.php/Je-LKS_EN/article/view/1130/1001

Cope, B., & Kalantzis, M. (2000). *Multiliteracies: Literacy learning and the design of social futures.* Psychology Press.

Cope, B., & Kalantzis, M. (2009). "Multiliteracies": New literacies, new learning. *Pedagogies: An International Journal, 4*(3), 164–195.

Cull, B. W. (2011). Reading revolutions: Online digital text and implications for reading in academe. *First Monday, 16*(6). http://pear.accc.uic.edu/ojs/index.php/fm/article/view/3340/2985

De Corte, E. (2016). Improving higher education students' learning proficiency by fostering their self-regulation skills. *European Review, 24*(02), 264–276.

Education world. (2016). Broadcast learning: The power of network learning. http://www.educationworld.com/a_tech/columnists/guhlin/guhlin003.shtml#sthash.GBQUyx3J.dpuf

Educause. (2016). Learning analytics. https://library.educause.edu/topics/teaching-and-learning/learning-analytics

Guhlin, M. (2012). Broadcast learning: The power of network learning. http://www.educationworld.com/a_tech/columnists/guhlin/guhlin003.shtml#sthash.GBQUyx3J.dpuf

Hayes, J. F., Maughan, D. L., & Grant-Peterkin, H. (2016). Interconnected or disconnected? Promotion of mental health and prevention of mental disorder in the digital age. *The British Journal of Psychiatry, 208*(3), 205–207.

Horizon reports. (2016). 2016 higher educational edition. https://library.educause.edu/~/media/files/library/2016/2/hr2016.pdf

Howe, N., & Strauss, W. (2000). *Millennials rising: The next great generation.* New York: Vintage Books.

Hutchins, R. M. (1969). *The learning society.* New York: New American Library.

ISTE. (2016). Here's how you teach innovative thinking. https://www.iste.org/explore/articleDetail?articleid=651&category=ISTE-Connects-blog&article=&utm_source=Twitter&utm_medium=Social&utm_campaign=MIXMEX

Ito, M., Horst, H. A., Bittanti, M., Stephenson, B. H., Lange, P. G., Pascoe, C. J., et al. (2009). *Living and learning with new media: Summary of findings from the Digital Youth Project.* MIT Press. http://files.eric.ed.gov/fulltext/ED536072.pdf

Jabr, F. (2013). The reading brain in the digital age: The science of paper versus screens. *Scientific American.* http://blogs.ethz.ch/wp-content/blogs.dir/976/files/2013/09/The-Reading-Brain-in-the-Digital-Age-The-Science-of-Paper-versus-Screens-Scientific-American.pdf

Koenig, S., Wolf, R., & Heisenberg, M. (2016). Vision in flies: Measuring the attention span. *PLoS ONE, 11*(2), 1–16. doi:10.1371/journal.pone.0148208

Laur, J., Schley, S., & Smith, B. (2006). *Learning for sustainability.* The Society for Organizational Learning (SoL) Inc.

Lenters, K. (2016). Telling "a story of somebody" through digital scrapbooking: A fourth grade multiliteracies project takes an affective turn. *Literacy Research and Instruction,* 1–22.

Luke, C. (2000). Cyberschooling and technological change: Multiliteracies for new times.

Lyashenko, M. S. (2016). Implementation of web-based technologies into teaching and learning practices in the university. *International Journal of Information and Education Technology, 6*(3), 243–246.

Majid, F. A., Mustafa, S. M. S., Jais, I. R. M., Shahril, W. N. E. H., Subramaniam, K., & Halim, M. A. A. (2016). A preliminary study on selected Malaysian millennials: Their characteristics and its implications on teaching innovation. In *Proceedings of the 7th International Conference on University Learning and Teaching (InCULT 2014)* (pp. 685–697). Singapore: Springer.

Noguchi, F., Guevara, J. R., & Yorozu, R. (2015). Lifelong learning for sustainable development. UNESCO Institute for lifelong learning. http://pie.pascalobservatory.org/sites/default/files/communities_in_action_-_lifelong_learning_for_sustainable_development.pdf/. Accessed April 01, 2016.

Oviatt, S. (2016). Computer interfaces can stimulate or undermine students' ability to think. In *Revolutionizing education with digital ink* (pp. 19–26). Springer.

Peters, O. (2000). Digital learning environments: New possibilities and opportunities. http://www.irrodl.org/index.php/irrodl/article/view/3/336

Prensky, M. (2000). Digital natives, digital immigrates. *On the Horizon, 9*(5), 1–6.

Prensky, M. (2001). Digital natives, digital immigrants do they really think differently? *On the Horizon, 9*(6), 1–6.

Ramakrishna, S. (2016). Strategies to be globally visible and locally engaged. *Drying Technology, 34*(3), 255–257. http://www.shanghairanking.com/wcu/wcu6/22.pdf

Sawyer, R. K. (2006). *The Cambridge handbook of the learning sciences.* New York: Cambridge University Press.

Scheunpflug, A., Krogull, S., & Franz, J. (2016). Understanding learning in world society: Qualitative reconstructive research in global learning and learning for sustainability. *International Journal of Development Education and Global Learning, 7*(3), 6–23.

Selber, S. (2004). *Multiliteracies for a digital age.* SIU Press.

Tapscott, D. (1998). *Growing up digital: The rise of the net generation.* New York: McGraw-Hill.

The New London Group. (1996). A pedagogy of multiliteracies: Designing social futures. *Harvard Educational Review, 66*(1), 60–93.

Visser, T. A. W. (2014). Evidence for deficits in the temporal attention span of poor readers. *PLoS ONE, 9*(3), 1–7. doi:10.1371/journal.pone.0091278

What is digital screen media? https://segd.org/what-digital-screen-media

What is the difference between an LCD and An LED backlit LCD display? http://www.makeuseof.com/tag/what-is-the-difference-between-an-lcd-and-an-led-backlit-lcd-display/

Wollscheid, S., Sjaastad, J., & Tømte, C. (2016). The impact of digital devices vs. Pen (cil) and paper on primary school students' writing skills—A research review. *Computers & Education, 95*, 19–35.

Chapter 4
Teacher-Centered Versus Learner-Centered Design of Screen

Content precedes design.
Design in the absence of content is not design, it's decoration.
Jeffrey Zeldman

Abstract In context of the Metasystems Learning Design Theory there are eight didactical systems. Each of these systems includes some elements of the teacher-centered and/or learner-centered learning environments. In plus, for the effective learning outcomes should be taking into account the specific features of that didactical system that may solve the previous identified issue. Thus, the specific features of the teacher-centered environments are: visibility, accessibility, language, readability, learnability, usability and legibility. Instead of this, the learner-centered are focused on developing knowledge, competence or/and self-regulated skills. The goal of this chapter is to describe the specific features of user interface design for the teacher-centered versus learner-centered learning environments.

Keywords Teacher-centered learning environment · Learner-centered learning environment

4.1 Introduction

User interface, by definition, is the aggregate of means by which users interact with a particular machine, device, computer program, or other thing. Generally, this is a widely term used to define the design principles of user interfaces for machines and software, such as computers, home appliances, mobile devices, and other digital devices. In the paradigm of Internet of Things and services there are a diversity of digital the screens and effects everywhere. Thus, the main focus of digital devices is on maximizing the user experience.

However, a specific feedback-feedward mechanism 'controls' the efficiency of all interfaces, allowing or blocking the capacity of human to proceed data,

© Springer Nature Singapore Pte Ltd. 2017
E.A. Railean, *User Interface Design of Digital Textbooks*,
Lecture Notes in Educational Technology, DOI 10.1007/978-981-10-2456-6_4

information and knowledge. First, this mechanism was managed by various inter-face elements, viewed on displaying component as:

– *input control* (buttons, text field, dropdown lists, toggles and others);
– *navigational components* (e.g. search field, pagination, tags and others);
– *informational-communication* (progress bar, notification, message boxes, windows).

All these elements are managed by mouse. However, when the user use portable devices and multi-touch screens add the value of the human's finger or/and voice for input, some principles of the interface design were changed. The problem is that new user interfaces become less intuitive. The mouse and touch input are so different. For example, the roll-over effects, that have a good impact on desktop computers, are less important on touchscreens. Further arguments to think about the user interface design is the vast difference in screen sizes.

Each time a user does not understand content presented on a screen, he/she can look around at the other information displayed in front or besider of him/her. Obviously, the size of the screen limits how can information can be read at once, before narrowing or enlarging the screen or scrolling down or up. Thus, the humans' capacity for information-communication, (meta)cognitive and assessment processes is determined by the dimensions of the screen. In plus, the attention span are also affected. It was observer, the bigger the screen size, the larger the capacity of the communication channel between the human and the screen. Maybe from this effect on actual learning through reading some children are trying to 'enlarge' the printed page. They cannot more proceed the information on the printed page because of text' size, graphic design and so on.

On the other hand, once students have to take action and navigate to a different view that their teachers (either by scrolling, enlarging, switching pages altogether etc.), they will incur an extra memory load. They must apply not all the techniques for reading, but also must remember the specific actions (e.g. how to open or close the screen/program, how to find/disseminate information that they need), as well as the specific Apps or/and tasks's combinations.

Third, the smaller screen size of the tablets or/and smartphones make the pro-vided content more difficult that desktop content. People usually 'use' working memory to keep information that may be available in future, but than, they doesn't authomatize knowledge to transform into a skill. However, the students may use the mobile devices not only for reading, but also to capture the image, to take a video, to download information or to send a message.

Fourth, the information that exists on digital screen are 'hyperlinked' with the information on other pages or/and environments. The simplest pattern is text plus animation or video games. If in the user interface design is used hyperlinks, the users should remember how to return back. This cause an extra load of the working memory and may be the reason of the distributive processing, and, therefore, to cause the attention' problem. As was noted by Harenberg et al. (2016), recent research demonstrate that video gaming can increase selective and distributive attention.

In a recent book Basar (2016, p. 159) describes about the plasticity of oscillatory behavior during the transition from the semantic memory to the episodic memory state. The preliminary results of transition between memory states emphases the fact that the reciprocal activation of the attention, perception, memory and remembering alliance is essential from the transition between two memory states. The problem is that digital screen easier activate the episodic memory that printed page, even it is displayed photos, animations, videos.

Fifth, the amount of information that actual students denote to a digital device is more than on printed pages. The attention capacity with a portable device is more different that on printed books/textbooks or computer display. In fact, the students are more interesting in a special device as a technological innovation, which on what Apps are installed and may be used for learning. They are more interested in looking on device, use as a phone or camera or, at least, to play a video game than to read a book or textbook. Does the digital content is important for learning, yet? If yes, how long is the average session duration on portable devices?

More specifically, for digital textbooks user interface design is the contact point of the author and his/her users. Nevertheless, who is the actual users and what design they need? In order to answer this question, we looked at the following definitions: (1) user interface design is the sum of information architecture; interaction design and visual design communications (Dragilev 2013) and (2) user interface design is a process that requires analyses of human performance and preferences, in particular the emotional and trust aspects of interaction (Dillon 2003, p. 457). In brief, the first definition views user interface design as a teacher-centered or goal-oriented approach. The second definition is focused on (meta)cognitive, affective, social and emotional aspects of self-regulated learning, e.g. this is the student-centered framework.

The student-centered interface design framework is a particular case of 'user-centered design', used to define a framework of processes (not restricted to interfaces or technologies) in which the needs, wants, and limitations of end users as a product, services or processes are given extensive attention at each stage of the design process. Therefore, the goal of student-centered interface design of digital textbooks is to anticipate what students might need to do for better results during learning or/and how to design interface elements that are easier to access, understand, and use in an affordable way for self-regulated learning.

Since 1970 a variety of tools, methodologies, models and instructions were proposed to make user interface design more easier and efficient. One of these is graphic design, which is communication design on the base on visual and textual content, focused on physical or/and virtual environments. Graphic design may include concepts and/or patterns from web design, interaction design, visual design, information architecture, instructional design of learning objects and learning design. However, this is not enough. The lack of transdisciplinary research focused on understanding how human' brain has been accommodated to the diversity of the learning environments for learning and what filters use for this, provide the situation when digital screens are everywhere, but their effects is more less than is expected.

The big diversity of concepts and/or patterns may be associated with design of teacher-centered and/or student-centered learning environment, and, therefore with user interface design of teacher-centered or student-centered functions of digital textbooks. Thus, the main functions of the school textbook with reference to teacher are: information, communication on the base on immediate/delayed feedback and reference (as a storage of data, information and knowledge). In addition, the main functions textbook with reference to student are: (meta)cognitive, affective, emotional and social purchases as well as consolidation and evaluation of purchases.

What we see now is a big divergence with above-mentioned ideas. In practice, user interfaces design, ranging from early requirements of educational software obsolescence to adaptive textbooks, has become a time-consuming and costly process. Most used is Graphic User Interface (GUI), which allows only exploring provided content through icons and other visual indicators. However, this is not enough because technology allow developing digital textbooks as text, audio or video; the text can be embodied also by the use in various formats, like graphic, animation, virtual reality and others. In addition, digital textbooks can be developed easier developed collaboratively and/or be disseminated through various user interfaces of digital devices like text-based, graphical, voice, kinetic, tangible, multimedia, multi-touch interfaces. To understand these challenges, more research is needed to investigate correlations between user interfaces design of digital textbooks and user interfaces design of digital devices.

User interface design is one of the most important and one of the most difficult issues in designing of the affordable digital textbooks. First, it is the 'contact point' between the user and the digital screen. Second, this contact point has a more large extent regarding to diversity of the learning environments, both real and virtual. Third, the users' capacity to proceed information is rapidly changing. There is no doubt that all these challenges will generate new research questions and demand decisions regarding what user interface design is better for learning.

This chapter is confronted with fundamental questions in user interface design of textbooks for teacher-centered and student-centered learning environments. The following models were considered: *affordance based design* (aims to analyse the users' needs, consider the affordance requirements of learning tasks, and identify the affordances of artefact components) and *ecological interface design* (aims to create advanced user interfaces for complex socio-technical system). In plus, common features of the *instructional design* and *learning design* aim to strength the application of paradigm for affordable user interface design of digital textbooks.

4.2 A New Context for Learning and Design Principles

In context of MetaSystems Learning Design Theory the context of learning correspond to the actual paradigm. Thus, the modelled context for learning must be placed in the learners' context (e.g. the knowledge, skills, and attitude). However, there are, at least, two different approaches for understanding the learning context.

One refers on conscious learning in schooling and the second is the unconscious or the hidden context for learning, which are every time and everywhere. But, how to understand the data used to generate the content for interfaces?

There are two controversial concepts: *instructional design*, building on the system theory and on the work of Dewey, Pappert, Bruner, Anderson and Thorndike etc., used to describe the potential use of machines in the classroom and *learning design,* used to describe a method of instruction for a particular peda-gogical session. As was noted by Scott et al. (2007) from the middle of 1990, the term *learning design* is associated with the design of learning utilised to facilitate learning. Does the learning design solved the issue of designing the hidden content for interfaces? If yes, why so many digital textbooks interfaces are so ineffective?

Designing of textbooks needs, also, to take into account the diversity of the digital screens and the human's capacity to work with information. In addition, designing a user interface for mobile devices is hard to do because some user interfaces are tiny, and some are larger. Today the learning designers are in the situation to design the textbook that should be affordable for reading on all devices. Different approaches to mobile design attempt to solve the problem of affordability in various ways. For example, if they are starting from the 4th industrial revolution principle of interoperability, then it is developed the idea of responsive design based on the relative priorities of the cells to be rearranged through a narrower communication.

Same content is available on various screens. However, the diversity of digital screens may affect the functionality of working memory. From one hand, the stu-dents have to work harder to keep more items in the memory, and from others—to understand how to work with the information provided on the screen. In the tra-ditional way, the students only read the content of textbooks (text and exercise). They used notebooks to solve the proposed tasks by the teacher. Digital textbooks, however, integrate informational-communication, (meta)cognitive and assessment processes and are, mainly for self-regulated learning. Some students may be willing to spend the time and effort within the learning environment with interactive assessment, adaptive content or pedagogical agents, others will simply give up (or be forced to give up) if they do not find what they need after a reasonable amount of time.

If the digital textbooks are not integrated with the curricula or some learning standards the learning outcomes will be very different. Therefore, the difficulties we face when learning with digital textbooks can fluctuate dramatically. Digital learning can vary from very easy to impossible hard. Reasons are variations in purchasing of knowledge, skills or competence; developing of skills; differences in required time and effort to understand the content. For examples, two or more frames or patterns may appear to have roughly similar amounts of information, but differ in the effort required to achieve performance for different learners.

Learning requires a dynamic and functional mechanism. Two learning mecha-nisms, described by Sweller (1994, p. 296) as the *schema acquisition* and *the transfer of learning procedures from controlled to automatic processing* are only a small component of the complex structure of the generative competence, where the schema is only the cognitive construct that could be been extended and automatized. In addition, information-communication, (meta)cognitive and assessment processes may be also taking into account.

According to ISO standard 52075, the design is based upon an explicit understanding of users, tasks and environments; users are involved throughout design and development; the design is driven and refined by user-centered evaluation; the process is iterative; the design addresses the whole user experience and the design team includes multidisciplinary skills and perspectives.

In use and development of digital textbooks, however, there are two main trends: teacher-centered and learner centered. If teacher directs the learning mechanism, that this is the teacher-centered mechanism, otherwise—this is learner-centered mechanism. The applicability of the user interface design principles for digital textbook design, first, depends on focus: teacher-centered interface design or user-centered interface design. Thus, teacher-centered interface design may be considered a framework of stages restricted to technologies in which it is important to follow the instructional objectives through stimulus, response and reinforcement. In contrast, in the learner-centered design a framework of activities or/and actions are not restricted to stimulus-response-reinforcement, but engage all students in a self-regulated learning process. The student may complete the provided content with own text, sketch, audio, video or animation.

Only one task is important for both cases: assessment, but this previous phase should be designed until the development or using digital textbooks, including open textbooks. There are some examples of questions for previous phase, as follows:

- What is the level of users' digital competence?
- What is (are) the user(s)' knowledge or skills level(s)?
- What difficulty of items are required?
- In which forms (open or/and closed) will be the students' answers?
- Which content does to be provided?

Therefore, these and other related questions are essential both for teacher-centered and learner-centered interface design. In designing is important to focus on a priori knowledge and skills, and to foster communication skills, taking into account the changing contexts for learning.

What is wrong with teacher-centered interface design? On the positive side, this approach has a long history in education and until it is a dominant vehicle for delivering knowledge on the base on curricula and instructional objectives. Practically, through the interface design of content is presented only the knowledge with details how to solve problems and, maybe, some interactive or adaptive tasks. On the negative side, however, the stimulus-response mode is the inadequate models of how students, with theoretical fundamentals based on theories of antiquity. This is inconsistent with current challenges of industrial revolution; e.g. nano-education, shifted communication methods, interoperability of contents, user generated content and others.

Fig. 4.1 Eight didactical systems

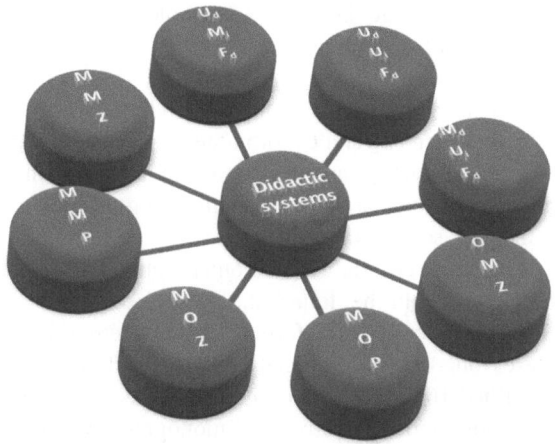

There is not empirical evidence that all teacher-centered interface design works well in all cases. There are, at least, eighth didactic models. If in the design is considered the criteria of communication, assimilation of knowledge and management of the learning process, than can be described eighth didactic models, as follows (Fig. 4.1).

Thus, the communication mode can be direct or indirect. In a direct communication style the truthfulness of knowledge are highly valued and to some extend are a higher priority that personal opinions or emotions. Saying *I don't know the answer* is considered a mistake since it goes to misunderstanding of the provided content. Problems are felt to be solved when the students know how to solve the academic problems or tasks. Open discussions are less encouraged, but are possible in an environment managed by the teacher. Instead, in the indirect communication style, negative information should be changed with the positive, and all tasks—with the solutions. In these situation, run away from the problem, which both parties usually knows the rules and recognize as such, are given, and in extreme cases are used a common strategy for learning (in our case it was the instructional dynamic and flexible strategy). All problems are felt to be solved more productively and, at the final stage, there are only solutions.

Moreover, either direct or indirect communication can be ensured through one (U_d and U_i) or more channels (M_d and M_i). However, the example of one channel can be printed text or audio text. Digital text refers to multi-channels or multimodal mode of communication. Digital 'extend' the features of the direct unimodal communication in favour of the multimodal communication. Thus, for example, a tablet for young children, encoded with the augmented reality drawings app, allow children to colour the characters that pop out of their books in real time. 3D printer has the potential to print the use interface in a new mode, used 'to synthesize' a three-dimensional object, previously modelled with the student(s). 3D glasses can be used to vision capacity of children through creating or enhancing the illusion of depth in an image. Does these technologies contribute to development of creativity or/and creative thinking?

Some ideas may come from the third criteria: management of provided knowledge. Thus, in the simplest mode the knowledge is communicated within a closed system (C_d and C_i) or in the open system (F_d or F_i). Digital textbooks within the closed system are developed on the base on educational system or state's conception, standards or/and methodology. In the open system there are only open standards, some tools and, maybe, design principles.

One more criteria will add other eight didactic schemas. Indeed, in the scientific literature could be found the Bespaliko (2002) description of the textbooks' diversity based on: aim, forms of learning environments, patterns and technology. If these four criteria are analysed on the bimodal diversity yes/no, than can be identified 16 types of the digital textbooks. Only on the aim level there are didactic, dogmatic, and declarative and monograph textbooks. The problem is that digital textbooks are developed as: *monographs* (e.g. eTextbooks, interactive textbooks, digital textbooks, adaptive textbooks etc.) and *dogmatic textbooks* (e.g. Cognitive Algebra).

However, only didactic textbooks (with or without the intelligent technological support) have the potential to improve self-regulated skills of the learner. A small remarks should be added for guaranteed result: instead of the didactic process should be considered the mathetics solutions for the previously identified tasks. Thus, user interface design of didactic digital textbooks are based on the didactic model that embodies information-communication, (meta)cognitive and assessment processes. The mechanism that ensure the functionality of the didactic model is the *instructional interactive and dynamic strategy*. Therefore, according to Metasystems Learning Design Theory, the instructional/learning/assessment strategy should allow students to develop self-regulated skills and teacher(s), to observe the synergetic effect within the dynamic development of the learning environment.

The results of the international survey prove, on average, that students view in digital textbooks the potential to develop and to increase the ability for self-regulate learning. This idea is based on acceptance the massive open online courses (MOOC), in which students are intrinsic motivated to learn new things in an individual way, in special when the computer based environment is extended at the global level. This means that students are interested to view on their digital screens only the short videos, but also the interactive tasks with immediate feedback and peer-to-peer assessment projects. They are less interesting to read digital text on the screen.

Let us consider a learning scenario that goes beyond the delivery method of knowledge. For example, a student sits at a digital screen on which new material is presented dynamically. The other student receive only one module, e.g. the *Introductory* module. The first student reads and take notes, highlighting the most important concepts/passages or finding the meaning of some concepts. The second student receives the module 'divided' into small frames following by tasks, developed on the base on Bloom, Simpson or other taxonomies. This student should complete the provided content at the level of synthesis (according to Bloom' taxonomy). Displayed content includes also a hidden content developed within the core concepts techniques (a case of concept mapping method). During the learning process she/he will receive multiple tasks, will exercise in a computer-based assessment environment; will complete the content with animation, 3D simulation etc., build own sketch or add photo/video/audio registration, and will ask teacher for some help. Which of these two models are better for learning?

Indeed, the delivered model of knowledge with teacher speech, or digital text, pictorial, adaptive or dynamic content does not improve learning substantially. Some improvement is possible, when students have the good capacity of short-term memory or working memory, and he/she is motivated enough to learn in a traditional way. Usually teachers indicate these students to use, also, a special form of assessment&assignments for better results during formative or/and summative assessment. However, when learning is an analysed only as a dynamic system, it is easy to observe that the number of students who are motivated to learn decrease considerable.

Many external influences cause the improvement or rejection the presented information on screen. Moreover, multiple digital screens distributed everywhere; maybe, affect students' perception. Thus, students unconsciously opens/close the 'cognitive filters' to protect the brain from the irrelevant, non-useful and non-interesting information. The other, not less important reason for accepted the virtual context for learning may be considered design norms that require less thinking effort, personalisation, messaging, self-directed activities in a more coloured and more attractive instead of bored activities with the printed textbooks environment.

4.3 Essential Elements in Teacher-Centered User Interface Design

Teacher-centered design is more a didactic process than a product. However, in the traditional way the process consists of some methods or techniques for constructing the instructional process within the practical application of one model. Where there are effective principles or/and standards that guide effective design, there is a certain amount of innovation and creativity in teaching/assessment processes. Whether or not the teacher-centered design is effective depends on the criteria used to define effectiveness.

By definition teacher-centered design focuses on teaching the knowledge. Theirs essential elements are visibility, accessibility, language, readability, learnability, usability and legibility.

Visibility is for setting up the instructional objectives and developing content to archive objectives through measurable outcomes. The most important indicator is what the student sees in the interface and how intuits the using of the interface. Therefore, good visibility is related on the things, objects, processes where everything is positioning in a way that can be easily found, used or intuit. The visibility property allows the author to show or to hide the text, rows or columns of a table while leaving the space. Thus, visibility is the property to see or to be seen.

Wang et al. (2004) describe that objective methods for assessing perceptual image quality traditionally attempt to quantify the visibility of errors (differences) between a distorted image and a reference image using a variety of known properties of the human visual system. Tan adds that poor visibility in due to the presence of some particles that have significant size and distribution in the participating medium. If the following is not taking into account, students involuntary will 'open' the cognitive filters to protect themselves. Thus, more research is needed to understand the functions, norms and correlations of design elements for visibility.

Korving et al. (2016) identify the relation between visibility and attention in weblectures. It was reported that students prefer weblectures with a visible lecturer to weblectures consisting of audio and slides only. Such preference is thought to be explained by the fact that selective attention is focused on relevant pieces of information in the process of understanding. Therefore, the visibility could be considered the degree in which a lecturer is visible in a weblecture. Focusing attention on an object, or thought, is considered to require attentional resources within the mind. More research is needed to understand the role of Gestalt principles and time.

Accessibility refers access to easy access to data, information and knowledge; intelligent tools or resource to find meaning of concepts. Some designers 'broke' the content into small pieces and offer students the possibility to interconnect pieces into a holistic whole. Others—design the interfaces that allow teacher to summarize various distributed contents into one. Lewthwaite and Sloan (2016) put the sign of equivalence between accessibility and permission, the interplay between operating systems and assistive technologies, browsing and other applications, the digital content and multimodal, flexible interactions. Accessibility requires a unique combination of theoretical understanding, as well as procedural and technical skills. It also draws from human-computer interactions, taking aspects of ergonomics and psychology to understand human characteristics and behavior, and disability studies, especially the factors that influence discrimination against people with disabilities and how discriminatory activity by individuals and organisations can be addressed.

According to Kumar and Owston (2016) there is a stringent need for innovative and assessable methods to ensure that students do not encounter any barriers in e-learning. Moore (2016) proposed to design inclusive features for simulations in chemistry in order to increase the accessibility of simulations both for teachers and for students, with and without disabilities. van Rooij and Zirkle (2016, p. 4) observe that in United States accessibility is governed by federal law, and, therefore, in all educational public institutions should be used the principles of the Universal Design, as follows: multiple modes of representation, multiple means of expression, and multiple means of engagement. The Universal Design norms enables creation of the accessible learning content for learners in all disability categories. Thus, the inclusive nature of the Universal Design and accessibility can enhance the learning experience of all learners.

Language of the digital textbooks interfaces is based on well-written texts in an academic way. However, there are not unique requirements of what language (e.g. teacher(s) or student(s)) to use. What is clear is that is not possible to opt out of using the technologic language instead of the academic language. On the other hand, it is impossible to ignore the technology for summarisation and dissemination of the content. First, the sentences should be simple, but with the possible 'extensions'. For example, student(s) receive the content and can complete this content with own text, video, video at the level of his/her understanding. From the other hand, the last know-how needed to deal with technologized forms of language is *multiliteracies*, since digital technologies. Therefore, rather that attempting to distinguish common features between printed and digital content and how to implement emotions in digital content, more important is to identify some conventions from earlier technologies.

The other issue is that digital screens, instead of printed, allow multiple forms of communications: direct and indirect, synchronic and asynchronic. These challenges change the nature of context for learning. Now, using digital devices it is easier to find any information. Thus, if student will have the option to choose between knowledge or skills, he/she will choose the second option. The worst thing is that in teacher-centered learning environment, the interfaces is not designed for learning, but for teaching and assessment.

The last, but not less important thing is that with digital interfaces may operate simultaneously in physical and symbolic spaces, learning or working simultaneously in different time zones, using typing and instant messaging instead of writing; swiping a screen or trackpad instead of turn the pages, speaking in a videoconference instead of presenting the portfolios. These actions require other meaning of language for design, because in the first case this is the language of activities, and in the second—the language of actions.

Usability defines how effective and satisfying it is for user to interact with the information presented on the screen. Challenges the way in which digital textbooks were situated as "supplementary" to an printed textbook can be considered a significant step toward the study of the learning design affordability. How quick and efficient can learner performs the assigned activities within the digital textbook environment? Is their same requirements for designing digital textbooks for a sustainable learning environment?

Many researchers note about the changing behaviours and perceptions of information during digital learning, like learner's culture, behavior patterns, learning styles, and motivation to learn. Some others proposed to use feedback in order to keep the communication patterns; to design relevant and consistent tasks and the efficient space for answer; to provide intuitive interfaces and to prevent errors by informing students of the specific features; to facilitate communication with the author of the content; to provide adaptive interfaces used for all in an efficient way. In plus, is important to keep the minimalist design in order to answer the question: What issues will be solved? Thus, the usability norms is when the

Table 4.1 Usability versus learnability within digital textbooks use and development

	Usability	Learnability
Definition	Extend on which a digital textbook can be developed and used to achieve the specific goals: efficiency, operability, attractive, memorability and untestable by the user, helpful to avoid errors, designed to safeguard the health	Intuitive interfaces, comprehensive input and output, as well as instructions readiness and messages readiness (when it is applicable). But, a learnable user interface can be very cumbersome for experienced users
Aim	To make possible for users to archive their goals when using the digital textbook as a pedagogical resource or tool for learning. Can the users accomplish their goal?	How easy is it for a user to learn how to use digital textbooks? How intuitive is interfaces to learn or to self-evaluate the knowledge?
Effect on the user	The more usable is the digital textbook, the more possible it is for a user to continue using the resourse/tool efficiently over long periods	The more learnable the digital textbook is, the less time the user takes in order to understood how to do a specific task withoud previous training and using any documentation

designed interface is equivalent to perceiving interface. The term 'usability' defines the degree of which the system can be used and with which it promotes learning and can be associate with the *learnability*, e.g. its efficiency, functionalities and others.

Learnability in teacher-centered learning environments refers on how well the designed activities enable obtaining guaranteed learning outcomes. To objective of learnability is to learn. Thus, the context with ambiguity of data provided by diversity of learning environments and the content, both in printed and digital forms, causes a contradictions regarding *what to learn* and *how to learn* for better memorisation, understanding and others. The differences between usability and learnability, according to international standards are, as follows (Table 4.1).

Some experts have classified learnability as an active component of usability (Cino and James 2016). According to ISO 9126-1 and 4 learnability is a subsystem of usability, along with understandability, operability, attractiveness and usability compliance. The learnability is a matter of how the possible futures making different hypotheses correct branch off from one another through time. The more complex the temporal entanglement of the futures satisfying incompatible hypotheses, the more difficult learning will be. Learnability is governed by the topological complexity of the possible hypotheses and computable learnability depends on their computational complexity.

Reliability is another concept that indicate to disposition to acquire new knowledge or skills over a broad range of relevantly possible environments. Reliability studiers are very diverse. For example, Topaloglu et al. (2016, p. 350) have equated software applications developed for web 2.0 with readable and writable web as well as with the possibility to develop information in a digital form and to share information around the world. Thus, the question comes up: To what purpose and why do teachers use digital textbooks? If the answer is: for teaching in an innovative way in a teacher-centered learning environment, than the reliability could be considered an equivalent of composing some distributed contents in a holistic one.

Solvability in a teacher-centered learning environment refers on an opportunity to develop an adequate strategy and prove that this strategy succeeds/not succeeds in the relevant sense. However, if the issue of solvability will be investigated from the cybernetic point of view, then it is used the algorithmic way. According to Gadouleau et al. (2016), the solvability problem asks whether the demands of all the destinations can be simultaneously satisfied by using linear network coding. The guessing number approach converts this problem to determining the number of fixed points of coding functions f: An → An over a finite alphabet A (usually referred to as Boolean networks if A = {0, 1}) with a given interaction graph, that describes which local functions depend on which variables.

Readability refers on the quality of writing that makes text easy or difficult to read and understand. The readability of text can be measured and improved. There are many tools and tests that can analysed the readability of the text. If the text is written in MS Word, the simplest way is to use the tool embodied in this program. For testing the readability it is used *Flesh Reading Ease, Flesch-Kincaid Grade Level, Gunning-Fog Index and others. Therefore,*

(1) <u>Fresh Reading Ease</u> test rates text on a 100-point scale, so that the higher the score, the easier it is to understand the document. The good readable text is when the score is between 60 and 70. The formula for the Flesch Reading Ease score is:

$$206.835 - (1.015 \times ASL) - (84.6 \times ASW), where:$$

ASL = average sentence length (the number of words divided by the number of sentences) and ASW = average number of syllables per word (the number of syllables divided by the number of words).

(2) <u>Flesch-Kincaid Grade Level</u> test aims to identify the readability of content at the school level. The formula for the Flesch-Kincaid Grade Level score is:

$$(0.39 \times ASL) + (11.8 \times ASW) - 15.59, where:$$

ASL = ave sentence length (the number of words divided by the number of sentences) and ASW = ave number of syllables per word (the number of syllables divided by the number of words).

In addition, many online tools allow testing the readability of the digital content. For example, using '*Readability Test*' can be calculated and interpreted the readability of digital textbooks, providing the website address.

Legibility is for quality of screen being clear enough to read. Ornamental fonts and text in all <u>capital letters</u> are hard to read, but italics and bolding can be helpful when used correctly. Large or small body text is also hard to read. Screen size of 10–12 pixel sans serif and 12–16 pixel serif is recommended. High figure-ground

Table 4.2 Topographic readability versus legibility

	Readability	Legibility
Definition	The way in which words and groups of words is arranged in a way that allows the readers eye to access the content easily and in a way that makes sense	The way of how a typeface is designed and how well one individual character can be distinguished from another
Specific features	*Spacing Height* (e.g. additional spacing placed before or after a paragraph) *Line Height* (e.g. if the line height of one paragraph is set to 2em and a paragraph is 1.5em, the first paragraph will require more paragraph spacing and probably more margins around it) *Size* (e.g. 13px or 0.813em at smallest) *Measure* (e.g. around 70 characters) *Letter spacing* (e.g. add generous letter spacing to subheads or phrases of uppercase text) *Good type contrast* *Successful hierarchy of contents* *digestible parts*	*Naturally open counters* (e.g. more words with o, e, c etc. help to define character is the most easiest way) *Individual letter shapes:* – large x-height can improve legibility – character shapes affect legibility *Serif typefaces:* lighter typefaces are usually more legible than heavier weights *Transparent type*: – content to be more important than the container

contrast between text and background increases legibility. Dark text against a light background is most legible (Table 4.2).

Affordability is the extent to which digital screen is affordable. Some digital screens is for presenting data, information or knowledge, others is for learning. In the first case, the students read the information, but in the second—need to spend time and effort to go through the content linearly or sequentially before they read any particular piece of information. Sometimes students may willing to spend the time and effort, but sometimes—not. How to facilitate the affordability of the digital screens for learning?

If one believes is important to offer direct access to content, making sure that navigation is easier. But, according to Barab and Squire (2004, p. 3), design-based research suggests a pragmatic philosophical underpinning, one in which the value of a theory lies in its ability to produce changes in the world. If so, we, as teachers, are in the core of global challenges for the sustainable development of students for better accommodation and relevant decision-making regarding the future of local and global world environment. In plus, textbooks designed for mobiles do take into account the limited channel capacity and make sure that students will learn. Mobile apps could add affordability of these textbooks, as apps around special tasks have built.

Alternatively, simply offering the indirect access through observing the student's behavior and helping them to develop own potential during learning. For this issue, some designers recommend to take into accord the interdependencies between

Table 4.3   Interdependencies between learner's need to learn and medium for learning

	Learner's need to learn	Medium
1.	Remembering a small amount of verbal information	Auditory medium
2.	Retaining information over longer periods of time	Textual information
3.	Learn information more effectively	Pictorial mode
4.	Recall and recognitize spatial relations in a story	Concept mapping
5.	Understanding motion-based information	Animation/video
6.	Difficult information, i.e. abstract concepts	Tool for exercising concepts
7.	Communicating verbal information	Textual information

learner's needs to learn and medium features that makes learning easier, as follows (Table 4.3).

There are many ideas how to develop rapid and intuitive user interfaces for learning. Google develops one of these apps, known as Primer. Nam (2015) has observed that only 3 % of people want to learn something new and spend own time during learning. Learning has several barriers to entry: you need to figure out what, where, how you want to learn, and then you need the time, money, and energy to follow through. In her opinion, digital screens designed for learning needed to be intuitive and inviting in order to overcome all factors that keep people from learning. Initially, the focus group has divided into three categories: *passive* (those who are looking around and browsing), *active* (that have more that an idea about what they want to learn) and *curious* (looking to learn something new, but not sure what). Then it was designed prototypes. There are three of the most important elements:

(1) *Dashboard*, e.g. lesson parks, letting users pick from three random lessons and others.
(2) *Lessons* with the rhythmically guide the user through the content.
(3) *Activities* with the three types of interactions that appears at different types, e.g. Quick Starts appear early in each lesson; Mid-Lesson Activities appear during the lesson; and Do This Nows come at the end.

This is an affordable model of the teacher-centered interfaces for learning.

4.4   Information Is Information, not Matter or Energy

'Information is information, not matter or energy'. This famous words of Wiener, written in 1948 for '*Cybernetics*: *Or the control and communication in the animal and the machine*' today is more important than even. We found this quote important for understanding challenges of the actual living and learning design. Does information, mater and energy are connected or not? This is the question of this paragraph.

We live in a globalized world in which 'reversing global climate change, pro-
tecting biodiversity, restoring the health of our oceans, developing sustainable food
systems, accelerating the shift toward clean, renewable energy—require funda-
mentally new ways of thinking and acting'. In such a word, teaching, assessment
and learning practice are 'integrated' with context, content, core competencies, and
habits of mind. Some of these practices could be extended on the base on innovative instructional strategies.

Can anybody learn something if he/she doesn't have a vital energy?

Can anybody learn something if he/she doesn't have a vital energy? Does the
human has a potential energy? What are the correlation between potential and
kinetic energy? How important is to use multisensory cues for changing potential
into kinetic energy? Is this process reversible or irreversible? What interface design
is the most important for deeper learning: those that organize information into
memorable 'chunks' or those that enable students in a dynamic self-directed
learning process? Some of the answers to these questions could be found in the
following article signed by Li et al. (2016, p. 65), as follows:

> Human beings' brains are one kind of high energy storage battery. Life is one procedure of
> studying. In the times of big data, the social network is incredibly growing, intelligence is
> increasingly increased, update periods of knowledge are becoming shorter and shorter, and
> new ideas and new knowledge are coming endlessly. Virtual learning, due to its advantages
> of quickly recharging brains, is being loved by people of all ages and levels. Nevertheless,
> community resident virtual learning autonomy requires cultivation.

It is a verified fact that everything is energy in motion, even the children
growing, reading, writing, recalling, emotions, memorisation, running, thoughts
and decision-making. All learning activities require energy. How about physiological actions or/and unconscious physiological functions, especially the role of
the unconscious affective reactions to deeper learning? Indeed, there are various
forms of energy important for learning: potential, mechanic, quantic and others.
But, not only the energy is important for learning (Fig. 4.2).

Therefore, energy is the condition for all the mechanic activities/actions, like
focusing attention on digital reading, walking during self-regulated learning, running away from classrooms and many others that students use to learn or to avoid
learning something new. Does these activities are initiated or activated by data,
metadata, information or knowledge provided or rapidly disseminated on/with
digital screens? Maybe yes, because digital screen instead of printed page are
working on/with energy. More research is needed to understand all these complex
and interconnected mechanisms, processes and stored data on the base on digital
screen.

The energy is at the head of the ancient medicine and cosmology. From the one
hand, the energy is vital for maintain all physical, mental and emotional activities
and actions of human body. Everybody 'vibrates' at some energetic frequencies
during his/her life. The brain's potential energy of processing data, metadata,
information and knowledge characterise the *learning style* (Keefe 1987; Reid 1987;
Riding and Sadler-Smith 1997), which associated with intellectual ability,

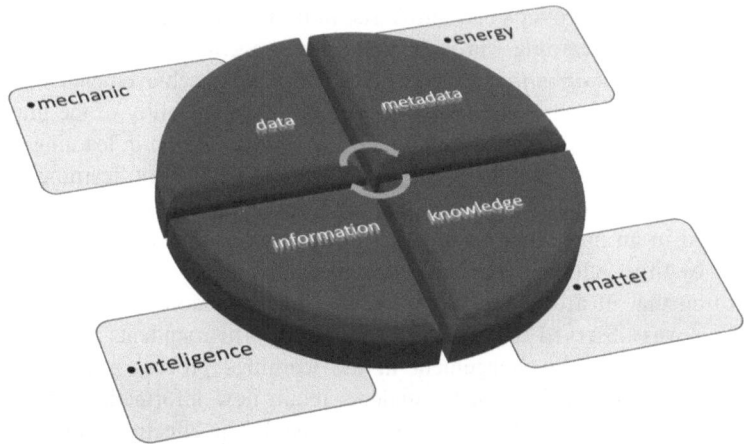

Fig. 4.2 The human body during learning

personality and achievement motivation, as was observed by Busato et al. (2000, p. 1057).

On other hand, digital interfaces attract people by 'default' rather than by deliberate choice. This is a kind of a new energy with the potential to motivate for sustainable understanding of the world, either real or virtual. What are the correlations between the brain and body' energy? Does the body energy is so important for identification, sorting, summarising things or patterns of the real world for decision-making? How important is the physical activity immediately after learning activity? Does sleeping improve deeper learning? These and many other questions should be answered before the scientists will be able to provide the adequate definition of what learning is?

Over the years, numerous studies of learning style and its multiple correlations with intellectual ability and educational outcomes show that learning style is a distinctive feature of learning preferences. Thus, according to Neuhauser (2010), the person who need people as a source for regenerating his/her energy is extroverted, whereas those who prefer solitude to recover energy may tend toward introversion. In plus, extroverts find their energy is sapped when they spend too much time along. Introverted people loss energy from being around people for long periods of time, particularly large crown. However, as was noted by Carl Jung, there is no such thing as a pure introvert or extrovert. According to Hans Eysenck, the differences between introverts and extroverts is a result of the extent (e.g. arousal) to which minds and bodies are alert and responsive to stimulus. In sum, several studies indicate difference between introverts and extroverts as correlations between arousal, learning, and memory (Eysenck 1976; Eysenck 2012; Swickert and Gilliland 1998).

Research has actually found that there is a difference in the human potential and capacity to learn in terms of how the information is processed and how the genetic makeup differs for extroverts and introverts. In turn, people learn from one another via *feeling* (e.g. learning through feeling); *recognizing* (e.g. patterns and meta-patterns); *memorization*, (e.g. artefacts). Learning achievements have reinforced within digital learning environment, thanks to availability of the immediate feedback. The drill and practice techniques is not yet a fashion in learning, even in learning mathematics, chemistry, physics. The affordance of learning through *repetitive practice,* when students receive small tasks for memorisation, should be investigated in an innovative manner. The learning, as repetitive actions, is characterized by time, effort, energy and intellect.

It is true that in a digital society, learning become more and more complex. Initially, it was observed that learning is effective when students are engaged in process and that active engagement in the learnings process promotes *mental activity.* The mental activity helps students retain new information and develop some *thinking capacities.* Therefore, it was proved that an effective learning process is individual, group based or collaborative. However, this is not enough for success in a digital society. In a powerful real-digital learning environment is required a mechanical-quantum energy for learning. The quantum energy is a result of *deeper thinking.*

The postmodern paradigm of learning should penetrate life deeper enough to answer essential questions of humanity and offer solutions for sustainable learning. Complicated problems cannot be solved at the same level as easy problems. For example, if the specific objective of learning is recalling the adding of numbers, then it is used immediate feedback. Thinking about learning from the paradigm of the human well-being is bound to give as a scare from the perspective of the understanding user interface design for a dynamic equilibrium of human life with the patterns of the UNIVERSE. To address an innovative learning paradigm it is required a new level of thinking about learning in general.

From the standpoint of the sustainable development, digital textbook is not digitalised/digitised version of printed textbook. Thus, there are no ultimate answer of what is the most effective methods for learning with textbooks. This mean that learning designers should move beyond the paradigm or develop instructional, assessment of learning model according to this paradigm. The provided 0model should be focused on solving the special task(s).

4.5   Essential Elements in Learner-Centered Interface Design

Learner-centered interface design refers on decide upon the look of a learner-centred learning environment that is vital for sustainable development and in which student(s) is central or became the central of own lifelong activities and/or actions for better adaptation in the local/global, or/and real/virtual challenges. He/she contribute to everyday decisions in the most rational way. Therefore, the learner-centered interfaces are developed together with the teacher during the learning process. Two remarks are important here, as follows:

- *By teacher*, we understand not only a person who teach, but also each of the resources, tools, phenomena, events, emotions, experience abroad into a on-formal or informal environments, which make learning possible.
- *By learning process*, we understood not only a component of a well-defined didactic process, but also the conscious and/or unconscious activities or/and actions of the brain which influence the behavior, during the assessment and thinking processes.

The most essential elements of the learner-centered learning environments are *core concepts* and interconnections between core concepts. The idea to use core concepts for learning design is proved by many transdisciplinary studies, including Fermi–Pasta–Ulam recurrence problem of non-linear systems; Pappert description of mathetics and so on.

Learning is both conscious and non-conscious, linear and non-linear. During learning is changed non only the synapses in the brain, but also the human body, the information, both mechanical and in forms of quantum waves that provide signals for learning and leaving. Maybe, digital screens form a special energetic cloud that 'make harder' for them learning in a traditional classroom or/with classical blackboard?

Theoretically, the formula for student's learning strategy can be described as $Y = D (X)$, where Y represent either a pedagogical or didactic goal; X—personal goal and D indicates the own strategy for learning used to transfer the pedagogical/didactic goal into a personalized goal. The limitation of formula is in formative self-assessment methodology. This idea is based on the assumption that computerised assessment exploits the feature of the digital content to be automatized through including into an interactive feedback and/or feedward loops and to be managed through a knowledge management model. From this perspectives, the nucleus of generative structure of competence operates as follows:

(1) The knowledge structure provided in the digital or multimodal content acts upon the human cognitive system at the level of goal-oriented influences and based on intellect, emotion, and energy at integrated (meta)cognitive, affective and psychomotor levels of competence.
(2) The incorporated tasks initiate the processes that are involved in acquiring the learning outcomes in transitory processes from the most current psycho-pedagogical state to the potential psycho-pedagogical state. The transition is equal to initial and final levels.

All psych pedagogical mechanisms of each learner are involved in these processes.

Into the dynamic and flexible instructional strategy all teaching, learning and assessment processes that lead to learning outcomes represent a hierarchical dynamic and flexible construct, developed by each student that are guided by a

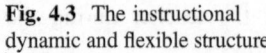 **Fig. 4.3** The instructional
dynamic and flexible structure

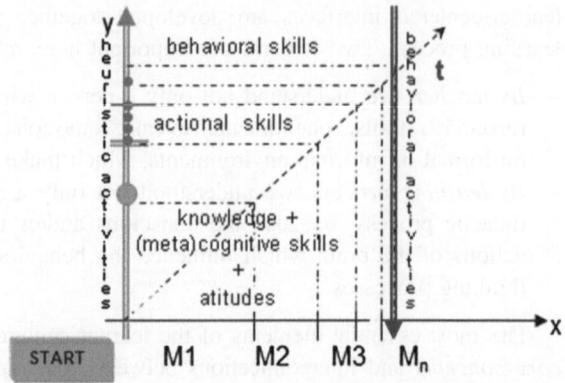

professional teacher. This is possible because the structure of content is generated
from an initial knowledge graph structure, which includes only interdependent
concepts. Each author of digital textbook can build the structure with interdepended
concepts, if he/she will use *concept mapping as* a technique for representing
concepts in knowledge graphs.

The methodological dimension is represented by the way, in which the didactic
process is integrated into functional structures that assure the efficiency of
communication/information, cognitive activity and assessment processes. The
proposed model is to consider the first phase equivalent to the first module, the
second phase-to the second module etc. Therefore, the digital content of the first
module incorporated from the reproductive (the content is recalled from the
memory) to productive tasks (the learner synthesis a new definition, concept etc. or
construct own content following concept mapping). The number of modules
depends on complexity or difficulty of concepts, but, in any case, it will serve as a
fundament for designing *learning tasks* and solving it in powerful learning environments. The graphic representation of "transfer" from pedagogical/didactic aim
into a personalized aim is reflected into an instructional dynamic and flexible
strategy, that reflect also the system of presentation the instructional content into
electronic textbook (Fig. 4.3).

The instructional dynamic and flexible structure shows an example of strategy that
ideally follows the principles of learner-centered learning environments. The content
of digital textbook is divided into *modules*. There are two possible models to present
digital content: *inductive* and *deductive*. Students learn effectively with either
inductive or deductive methods. The content of each module is structured around
information framework with formative assessment tasks and concept mapping tool.
In time the number of *algorithmic activities* tasks, focused on reproductive skills,
decrease in favour of *heuristic activities*. In an algorithmic method, the student is
presented with all data for problem-solving, context and procedures are described.
The learner's decision is based on understanding and reproduction of presented
algorithm. However, during heuristic activities step-by-step procedures of learning
are not provided or explained explicitly.

References

Barab, S., & Squire, K. (2004). Design-based research: Putting a stake in the ground. *The Journal of the Learning Sciences, 13*(1), 1–14.

Basar, E. (2016). *Memory and brain dynamics: Oscillations integrating attention, perception, learning, and memory.* CRC Press

Busato, V. V., Prins, F. J., Elshout, J. J., & Hamaker, C. (2000). Intellectual ability, learning style, personality, achievement motivation and academic success of psychology students in higher education. *Personality and Individual Differences, 29*(6), 1057–1068.

Cino, D., & James, T. (2016). A Usability and Learnability Case Study of Glass Flight Deck Interfaces and Pilot Interactions through Scenario-based Training.

Dillon, A. (2003). User interface design. *Encyclopedia of Cognitive Science* (Vol. 4, pp. 453–458). London: MacMillan.

Dragilev, D. (2013). What is User Interface Design? http://www.freshtilledsoil.com/what-is-user-interface-design/

Education for a Sustainable Future. Benchmarks for Individual and Social Learning. http://www.susted.com/wordpress/wp-content/uploads/2016/04/Benchmarks-Draft-Final-5.pdf

Elias, T. (2011). Universal instructional design principles for mobile learning. *The International Review of Research in Open and Distributed Learning, 12*(2), 143–156. http://www.irrodl.org/index.php/irrodl/article/view/965/1675

Eysenck, M. W. (1976). Arousal, learning, and memory. *Psychological Bulletin, 83*(3), 389–404.

Eysenck, M. (2012). *Attention and arousal: Cognition and performance.* Springer Science & Business Media.

Gadouleau, M., Richard, A., & Fanchon, E. (2016). Reduction and fixed points of boolean networks and linear network coding solvability. *IEEE Transactions on Information Theory, 62*(5), 2504–2519.

Haley, A. (2016). It's about legibility. https://www.fonts.com/content/learning/fontology/level-4/fine-typography/legibility

Harenberg, S., McCaffrey, R., Butz, M., Post, D., Howlett, J., Dorsch, K. D., et al. (2016). Can multiple object tracking predict laparoscopic surgical skills? *Journal of surgical education, 73*(3), 386–390.

Human-centred design for interactive systems (ISO 9241-210, 2010). http://www.iso.org/iso/catalogue_detail.htm?csnumber=52075

Keefe, J. W. (1987). Learning Style Theory and Practice. National Association of Secondary School Principals, 1904 Association Dr., Reston, VA 22091.

Kelly, K. T. (2016). Learning theory and epistemology. In *Readings in Formal Epistemology* (pp. 695–716). Springer International Publishing. http://repository.cmu.edu/cgi/viewcontent.cgi?article=1383&context=philosophy.

Korving, H., Hernández, M., & De Groot, E. (2016). Look at me and pay attention! A study on the relation between visibility and attention in weblectures. *Computers & Education, 94*, 151–161.

Kumar, K. L., & Owston, R. (2016). Evaluating e-learning accessibility by automated and student-centered methods. *Educational Technology Research and Development, 64*(2), 263–283.

Lee, A., & Lochovsky, F. H. (1985). User interface design. *Office automation* (pp. 3–20). Berlin: Springer.

Lewthwaite, S., & Sloan, D. (2016). Exploring pedagogical culture for accessibility education in Computing Science. http://eprints.soton.ac.uk/388799/3/Lewthwaite-Sloan-w4a2016-camera-ready.pdf

Li, F., Xue, Q., Zhang, H., & Deng, E. (2016). How to Improve Community Resident Autonomous Learning Based on Virtual Learning. *International Management Review, 12*(1). http://scholarspress.us/journals/IMR/pdf/IMR-1-2016/IMR-v12n1art7.pdf

Lindemann, P. (2016). A Short Report on Multi-Touch User Interfaces. https://www.medien.ifi.lmu.de/lehre/ws1011/mmi2/mmi2_uebungsblatt1_loesung_lindemann.pdf

Moore, E. B. (2016). ConfChem conference on interactive visualizations for chemistry teaching and learning: Accessibility for PhET interactive simulations progress, challenges, and potential. *Journal of Chemical Education.*

Multimedia User Interface Content. http://www-i4.informatik.rwth-aachen.de/content/teaching/lectures/sub/mms/mmsSS02/slides/13.pdf

Nam, S. (2015). Making learning easy by design. https://medium.com/google-design/designing-a-ux-for-learning-ebed4fa0a798#.9suxjluob

Neuhauser, C. (2010). Learning style and effectiveness of online and face-to-face instruction. *The American Journal of Distance Education*, 99–113. http://web.cerritos.edu/nbueno/SitePages/Pepperdine/Learning%20Style%20and%20effectiveness%20and%20online.pdf.

Oppermann, R. (2002). User-interface design. In *Handbook on information technologies for education and training* (pp. 233–248). Berlin: Springer.

Pallotta, V., Bruegger, P. Hirsbrunner, B. (2008). Kinetic user interfaces: Physical embodied interaction with mobile pervasive computing systems. In *Advances in Ubiquitous Computing: Future Paradigms and Directions*, IGI Publishing, February, 2008. http://www.igi-global.com/books/additional.asp?id=7314&title=Preface&col=preface

Readability Test. http://juicystudio.com/services/readability.php

Reid, J. M. (1987). The learning style preferences of ESL students. *TESOL Quarterly, 21*(1), 87–111.

Riding, R. J., & Sadler-Smith, E. (1997). Cognitive style and learning strategies: Some implications for training design. *International Journal of Training and Development, 1*(3), 199–208.

Scott, B., Shurville, S., Maclean, P., Cong, C. (2007). Cybernetic principles for learning design. http://www.univie.ac.at/constructivism/archive/fulltexts/1796.pdf

Sweller, J. (1994). Cognitive load theory, learning difficulty, and instructional design. *Learning and instruction, 4*(4), 295–312.

Swickert, R. J., & Gilliland, K. (1998). Relationship between the brainstem auditory evoked response and extraversion, impulsivity, and sociability. *Journal of Research in Personality, 32*(3), 314–330.

Tidwell, J. (2010). *Designing interfaces*. O'Reilly Media, Inc.

Topaloglu, M., Caldibi, E., & Oge, G. (2016). The scale for the individual and social impact of students' social network use: The validity and reliability studies. *Computers in Human Behavior, 61*, 350–356.

Typographic Readability and Legibility. http://webdesign.tutsplus.com/articles/typographic-readability-and-legibility–webdesign-12211

van Rooij, S. W., & Zirkle, K. (2016). Balancing pedagogy, student readiness and accessibility: A case study in collaborative online course development. *The Internet and Higher Education, 28*, 1–7.

Wang, Z., Bovik, A. C., Sheikh, H. R., & Simoncelli, E. P. (2004). Image quality assessment: From error visibility to structural similarity. *IEEE Transactions on Image Processing, 13*(4), 600–612.

Chapter 5
Knowledge Ecology and Sustainable Development

You can't teach people everything they need to know.
The best you can do is position them where they can find
what they need to know when they need to know it.

Seymour Papert

Abstract Knowledge ecology refer on the investigation and epistemological theorizing various ways of knowing and sustainable development. Although fourth industrial revolution is coming, the pedagogy is seeking to maintain old theoretical concepts and methods. This cause a dialectical contradiction between requirements of living in a real world for sustainability, philosophy of scientific transhumanism and current education. It is not so important for pedagogy to be the art of teaching. It is a stringent need for pedagogy to become the science that deals with identification and solving controversies, problems and issues, related on sustainable development. The goal of this chapter is to describe the user interface design principles of digital textbooks from the perspective of knowledge ecology and scientific transhumanism.

Keywords Knowledge ecology · Scientific transhumanism · Principles

5.1 Introduction

The term 'knowledge ecology' refers on investigation and epistemological theorizing the various ways of knowing for sustainable development. In concept of Metasystems Learning Design Theory, the knowledge ecology is an equivalent to application of the ergonomic principles. On one hand, it denotes the interconnections of fundamental principles from philosophy, psychology, pedagogy, neuroscience, management, cybernetics and educational technology at the level of 4th industrial revolution. And on the others that 'research at and beyond the frontier of understanding is an intrinsically risky venture, progressing in new and the most exiting research areas and is characterised by the absence of disciplinary boundaries' (ERC 2016). Therefore, if we intent to develop affordable solutions for

© Springer Nature Singapore Pte Ltd. 2017
E.A. Railean, *User Interface Design of Digital Textbooks*,
Lecture Notes in Educational Technology, DOI 10.1007/978-981-10-2456-6_5

learning with digital textbooks, only the frontier research in pedagogy is effective to understand user-interface design.

What are these principles? In order to understand this question let us to analyse certain principles of the fourth industrial revolution and theirs affect education. According to Gandhi (2015) 4th industrial revolution is guided by: *interoperability*; *virtualization*; *decentralization*; *real-time capability*, *service orientation* and *modularity*. But, from the MetaSystems Learning Design Theory approach, that it is focused on learning, the results indicate to self-regulation, personalisation, clarity, dynamicity and flexibility, ergonomics and feedback.

In both cases, the principles of 4th industrial revolution indicate to the need of an innovative structure of competence, which is generative enough to be 'extended' during all life. From the pedagogical point of view, this means developing the student's strategy on the base on developing/extended knowledge, skills and attitudes. What does this combination of the principles from various domains and the direction of movement of informational-communicational technologies for education mean for learning designer?

The reorientation of educational technology toward the knowledge ecology is a key link between each human individuality and required generative structure of competence for future rapid adaptation to all challenges during the life. Fourth industrial revolution is on the way. Schwab (2016) notes that it is already created radically new approaches that revolutionized the way in which individuals and institutions engage and collaborate. On-demand economy within technology based platforms makes possible to manage many things using a smart phone, e.g. convene people, assists and data and create a new ways of goods and services like 3D printing or using the voice on the Google app or Chrome to search, get directions, and create reminders.

For the actual pedagogy, digitization and on-demand economy enables to use educational platforms for learning or platforms for downloading, reading, disseminating or/and collaborative development of the online textbooks. The common thing of the most technology platforms is the descriptive power of openness and accessibility (e.g. lost cost, the courses provided by the best universities etc.). However, these platforms function in other way, seeding trust for innovation in order to changes traditional conceptualisation of didactics. This is also a new call for mathetics, as sciences of the problems in/for learning and its practical solutions.

Fourth industrial revolution is forcing all educational systems to re-examine the way they provide learning. Major impacts of the actual phase are dealing with expectations on education 3.0 paradigm to value nano-learning, networking, sustainable development and lifelong learning. But, how to develop skills with a chaotic distributive knowledge and without own attitude for learning? Major impacts—teacher expectations of environment for learning are shifting—classrooms are being enhanced by interactive whiteboards, which improves digital competence both of students and teachers—new methods of learning are being formed as teachers learn the importance of new forms of teaching, learning and assessment and—digital textbooks are being transformed into new digital models.

Diversity of screens are increasingly at the centre of the digital revolution, which now are everywhere. However, students expect to gain practical experience and that, looking for new opportunities (knowledge, skills, attitudes), they entered in the virtual world. There, they are more extrinsic motivated and self-regulated in order to develop some practical skills for lifelong learning. These students can be identified based on their willingness and digital skills to find new information, to share digital data and interact. They don't want to learn when teachers use the classic methodology for teaching. From the technological point of view, the educational system is moving much more to peer-to-peer sharing and personalised content than on personalised nano-education. We are living in a world, which requires pedagogy to respond in real time wherever it is or their teachers or/and students may be.

In sum, students who used digital devices for learning could have obtained better educational outcomes, if they a good memory and same digital skills. In other cases, skills should be developed with adequate pedagogy. However, many schools around the world is seeking to maintain old theoretical concepts and methods. This cause a dialectical contradiction between requirements of living in a real world, philosophy of scientific transhumanism and pedagogy. In the simplest form of this thinking, we can hear everywhere that pedagogy is not a science. In a more complicated form, teacher training is neglected at all or, at least is very formal, especially in the field of trans-disciplinary frontier research.

Critics of digital learning suggest, that screens don't allow children learn. Indeed, if at the front of the class is an old-fashioned blackboard, but in the hands of are digital devices and outside off school—a diversity of digital screens, these cause a confusion for processing information. Brand cannot identify the right way, and therefore, makes a lot of investigations and copies. But, what is the correlation between real world and the virtual reality? How to make a difference and/or how to integrate them in a holistic whole for an adequate decision? How to think in a new environment using/without using a digital device?

Now, the investigation of the learning mechanisms, decision-making strategies and other more complex issues is more important than even, but such investigations should be focused on developing the metasystems thinking. There are many projects everywhere, showing that learning is both conscious and unconscious. The brain chooses the decision for one or other situation in dependence on available schemas and networking. Many decisions requires time. In this context, the knowledge ecology, based on MetaSystems Learning Design Theory, aims to identify the right strategy (or methodology, methods, procedure, and technique) to learn from the availability plethora of ways for knowing, like resources, tools, patterns etc.

All environments, either real or virtual, local or global, open or closed are the learning environments. We learn everytime and everywhere, even during sleeping. In brief, the diversity of learning environments could be classified in two categories: *teacher-centered learning environments* and *learner-centered learning environments*, including all possible combinations ranging from 100 to 0 % implications of teacher (Fig. 5.1).

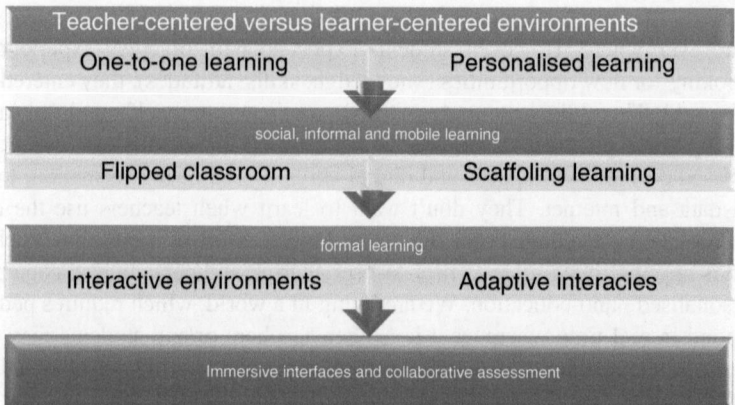

Fig. 5.1 The diversity of the user interfaces for learning

Instead of the traditional classroom, when learning is only the equivalent of reading, writing and problem-solving, in the actual society there are many other environments. These distributed environments are real or virtual, and the problem for education is that there are more creative that those proposed by the actual teachers. Therefore, screens with attractive user interfaces are located everywhere and are available everytime. What are the students' activities and/or actions on these screens that provided various and, usually irrelevant for required data, metadata, information and knowledge for learning?

In concept of the MetaSystems Learning Design Theory learning is a complex mechanism than embody various resources and processes, (meta)cognitive, emotional and affective reactions, conscious and un-conscious activities and decisions, as well as psychological, physiological, psychic and other behavioural actions. The learning occurs both in real and virtual, local and global environments. Instead of pedagogical system, that is a closed system, the learning environments in the Age of both fourth industrial and cognitive revolutions are more open and flexible. The most important outcomes is *generative structure of competence*.

The generative structure of competence is on the fundaments of the 'flexible, dynamic and instructional strategy' (Railean 2008). This strategy indicates on powerful learning environment; in which learning is focused on competence development through developing own digital textbooks. A strategic procedure is required to grown perfect crystals. One can observe that "crystal" is similar to the learning outcomes and the process of growing the crystal could be associated with learning. This similarity allows predicting that powerful learning environment is like a saturated solution needed at the beginning of crystal growing process. This solution needs to pour over a substrate, which in our case, corresponds to context for learning.

First, it is important to obtain a "seed crystal". In our case we will "concentrate" the main concepts in module I and, at the final phase, will add a quiz. After student wills successful pass the quiz, he/she will be engaged in active personalized learning with formative assessment and peer evaluation of project. Our "crystal" will grow! At the end of the learning process we can keep our crystal in a closed container or will "cover with a protective solution" (in our case, this is a certificate) for future exploration.

What norms and methods are better in order to achieve the estimated outcomes for learning? What interfaces should be designed for learning "crystal" how to grow? In order to understand the answer on these questions let us 'divide' the methods into three plus one category. Thus, the first module is for one-to-one and personalised learning; the second module—is for scaffolding and blended learning and the third module—is for immersive learning and collaborative assessment.

5.2 One-to-One or/and Personalised Learning?

One-to-one learning refers to one of the following metaphors: 'one computer for every student'; 'one-to-one tutoring'; 'one-to-one initiative', 'one-to-one instruction', 'one-to-one laptop programs' and many others programs, methods or techniques. Personalised learning refers on student's strategy that is focused on solving the real issues during the learning in an optimized way. Both, on-to-one and personalised learning is an alternative to traditional approaches to teaching in which teacher with/without textbooks provide all students in a given lesson or course the same type of instruction, assessment, recommendations for better learning.

Both one-to-one learning and personalised learning interfaces can be designed for learner-centered environments. However, the general goal of personalisation is to make individual learning needs the primary consideration of teacher, instead of one-to-one learning, when is more important the learning styles. The problem is that in the literature is described many examples of successful personalised learning environments in real/virtual, but without any theoretical argumentations. For example, Salmon et al. (2016, p. 208) notes, as follows.

In order to provide a personalised, engaging experience, <...> have maintained an active online presence, often setting up discussion threads with provocations, encouragement and questions. The timing and distribution of forum posts was critical also. Regular personalised emails were also sent to touch base with individuals, to build a relationship, and to respond to their individual needs.

What are the specific features of one-to-one and personalised learning? Are there any differences in the evolution of one-to-one and personalised learning concepts? One-to-one learning is considered the first special teaching method when a passionate student comes to a teacher and asked to be learn in an individual way. This seems to be a challenging situation for programmed textbooks to be the right resources both for one-to-one and personalised learning. Apart from the Skinner's book: *The Science of Learning and the Art of Teaching*, on looking through instructional design of the digital textbooks interfaces only sometimes can be identified any sections on teaching one-to-one learning and/or those that are personalised as a mechanic assembling of the digital pages. It was somehow assumed that one-to-one learning with a digital interfaces means organising programmed instruction, while the reality is that one-to-one is a significant part of the didactic process may improve learning, and, therefore, should be identified the suitable conditions to achieve this result.

According to Lockee et al. (2016, p. 546), the school did not pay attention to the contingencies of reinforcement; for those students who did get answers correct, many minutes to several days may elapse before papers are corrected. This is a particular problem for children in the early stages of learning who depend on the teacher for the reinforcement of being right as opposed to older learners who are able to check their own work. In plus, starting from the actual educational paradigm could be observed that digital assessment norms differ by paper-pencil assessment norms. Controversial topics such as students' learning pattern versus environmental multi-patterning, reproductive versus productive tasking, digital assessment timing and scheduling have often been misunderstood. Usually, in a learner-centered environment the student is asked not to reproduce, but to produce and share knowledge. Can be digital interfaces used to automatize core concepts?

All above-mentioned questions have solutions, if user interfaces for learning will be understood not only as for listening, recalling, writing processes or making calculus, but also be planned at the level of the paradigm and technological achievements at which learning is required. For example, listening in a digital learning environment is a more active learning process then in a classroom, if in the second case is used traditional methodologies. The other example is broadcast learning. The broadcast learning, as was noted by Guhlin (2002), aims to built-in video camera directly at the speaker, announce the availability of the presentation on the e-mail list and chat about what was going on or broadcasting a spotlight speaking presentation with colleague to a worldwide audience that share their knowledge on the topic.

The listening skills may be increased through broadcast learning. There are two way: unidirectional and multi-directional. There are a variety of tools that may be embodied in interface design of digital textbooks and used for multi-directional broadcast, for example in learning foreign language, most of them involving access to a computer that has built-in video camera and a microphone. In minutes, the content of the digital textbooks can be broadcasting, even via wireless connection, to a worldwide audience. For these propose are available two types of solutions, (a) those hosted by third party providers and (b) those that user host yourself on own server. Some of them related on free hosted solutions, like UStream.tv, E2BN FlashMeeting, Blip.tv and Kyte.tv, but some are commercial, such as Persony.com and Yugma.com.

One practical example was describes in the literature. For interactive broadcasting learning were used UStream.tv and Moodle with DimDim installed. The UStream.tv was used for conference been considered the easiest way to engage students in learning, while Moodle with DimDim was the solution that allows control over the content, hold meetings online with a chat component. It is recommended, that the speaker will actively use built-in chat technologies or Twitter as a way of keeping in touch with the audience; to assign a moderator who will serve as the liaison from the audience at-large to the presenter/speaker.

5.3 Blended, Flipped or 'Scaffolding' Interfaces for Learning?

While no standardized approach exists for the design of user interface design of digital textbooks, some commonalities across flipped and scaffolding interfaces can be identified. Therefore, according to Network (2014), the flipped learning is a pedagogical approach in which direct instruction moves from the group learning space to the individual learning space, and the resulting group space is transformed into a dynamic, interactive learning environment where the educator guides students as they apply concepts and engage creatively in the subject matter. There are four pillars of flipped learning (Fig. 5.2).

What interfaces are required for flipped learning? The problem is in transformative changing from the group learning space (e.g. classic didactic model) to direct instruction (e.g. one-to-one learning, personalised learning etc.) that requires knowing what is and how to apply knowledge, (meta)cognitive skills and attitudes. Next successful steps in learning requires practical application of actional and behavioural skills. Does scaffolding be a solution? According to the Glossary of the Educational Reform, scaffolding refers to a variety of instructional techniques used to move students progressively toward stronger understanding and, ultimately, greater independence in the learning process. During scaffolding, teacher provides

Fig. 5.2 Four pillars of flipped learning. Adapted from Network (2014)

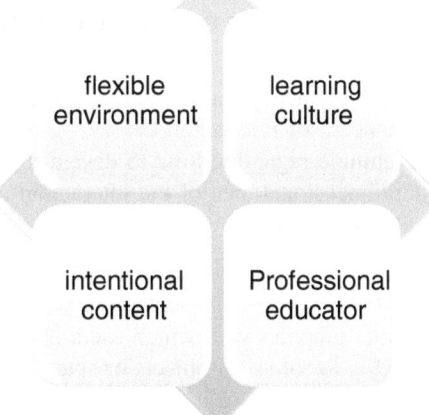

flexible environment

learning culture

intentional content

Professional educator

successive levels of temporary support that helps students reach higher levels of comprehension and skill acquisition that they will not archive without assistance.

Sedig et al. (2001) guide even expresses reluctance to define the role of interface manipulation style on reflective cognition and concept mapping, stating the role of three interfaces: (a) *Direct Object Manipulation* interface; (b) Reflective Direct Concept Manipulation (RDCM) interface and (c) *Direct Concept Manipulation* interface that is extended with scaffolding. All these interfaces to design for students to process information consciously were used. But, dispute the relative difficulty when using the interface studies it was proved that interface designed for scaffolding are more focused on reflective cognition and deep learning.

From one hand, the practical application of the scaffolding to learning is to 'scaffold' students' reading, writing or making calculus experiences by letting teachers embed annotations, multimedia, 'checkpoint' questions, and formal assessments that can prompt students to consider key points, offer alternative way of interacting with the text and prove for understanding. From the other hand, scaffolding could be designed as an interactive, dynamic and flexible model of learning, in which learner gains knowledge, develop/increases skills and obtain own attitudes regarding phenomena, mechanisms, processes and learning objects around them.

Now, within the digital learning environment, the scaffolding techniques may be associated with a blended learning techniques, which offer multiple yields when delivery the right content for learning. Usually, blended interfaces are used in the flipped classroom in order to archive an active learning component. There are two more design questions needed to be solved before decide what model is better: blended, flipped or 'scaffolding' interfaces for learning. The first question relies on identification the right techniques for optimization the content that will be delivered for learning, because it is not so important what type of technology will be used to deliver the content, most important what and for what reason will be delivered.

5.4 Interactive or Adaptive Interfaces for Learning?

Digital interfaces are more interactive and/or adaptive. The interactive interfaces is the concern of *interaction design*—a blended endeavor of process, methodology, and attitude regarding how to design the interactive environments. Analysing the multidimensional area of the interaction design language, Silver (2007) identified five dimensions, e.g.

- 1D is for words as interactions;
- 2D is for visual representations, which include typography, diagrams, icons, and other graphics with which users interact;
- 3D is for physical objects or space *with* which or *within* which users interact;
- 4D is for time *within* which users interact—for example, content that changes over time such as sound, video, or animation;

- 5D is for designing a behavior, including action, or operation, and presentation, or reaction;

This list could be continued, as follows. Therefore,

- 6D is for designing adaptive behavior, including adaptive learning environments, systems, cognitive mechanisms and/or (meta)cognitive and adaptive processes;
- 7D is for sustainable education, including designing learning environments for sustainability; metasystems, special learning tools and open resources.

These interaction design languages impact development the interactive and/or *adaptive interfaces* for learning, which is important for some specific learning outcomes. Sceptics believe adaptive digital interfaces are not so important for learning. They embody Apps into traditional designed content and hope that this is more important than adaptive interfaces.

However, advocates of adaptive interfaces found that compared to traditional or video versions of traditional lectures, blended and flipped courses with the adaptive software produced higher scores on summative evaluation. In plus, as was indicated by Browne et al. (2016, p. 8) describes the results of the *Adaptive Intelligent Dialogues* project aims to research and develop techniques for designing and building adaptive computer interfaces note that the term adaptive refers both to self-adaptive and user tailored systems. It was recognized that adaptiveness is required in the interface because no single fixed solution is suitable for all users or even one user over the period or range of applications. In plus, the interfaces need to adapt to the users' changing skills and requirements and the assistance provided by the system needs to be relevant to the task the user is performed. However, these requirements were important until the second digital revolution. Regarding the self-adaptive interface, it was identified three types, as follows (Fig. 5.3).

The main feature in adaptive interface design is the dialogue on *immediate feedback*. There are multiple patterns used to achieve adaptively with or without Artificial Intelligence techniques. But, if we intent to understand what types of adaptive interfaces are important for learning, initially we should understand why is

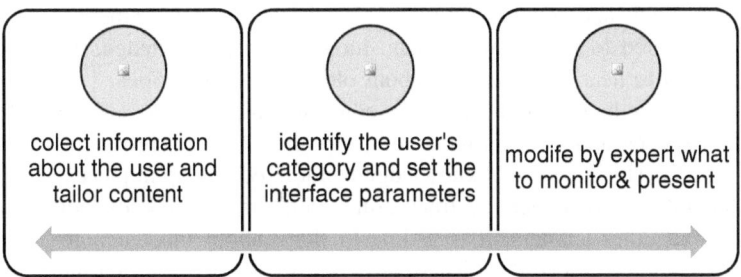

Fig. 5.3 Interconnections of self-adaptive interfaces

important to develop adaptive systems and what systems are more affordable: interactive or adaptive.

Most computer adaptive systems intend to teach the heterogeneous end-users. However, in proposed design models the content is only tailored to students' knowledge, preferences, learning styles and so on. This is the industrial case when various sizes of one model increase its potential market. Nevertheless, there is a limitation of how much individuality and flexibility can be incorporated into one educational software.

Weber and Brusilovsky (2016) described the system ELM-ART aims to support new students in their first steps of learning in a new domain within a more valuable way through carrying novice learners for mastering the next steps with a good textbooks and well selected examples. In the authors point of view, ELM-ART opened the way for future generations of open adaptive and intelligent textbooks that could be gradually expanded integrating new content and new learning activities produced by a broad community of practice.

The situation is not similar in design and development of the adaptive textbooks, described by other authors. As was noted by Kostolányová and Šarmanová (2016), the creation of adaptive textbooks is more demanding than the production of classic e-learning textbooks and that to have a classic textbook, as a source for production adaptive textbooks is desirable. More important is streamlining of the education process through individualisation that will allow acquiring the knowledge in a more natural way (personally tailored for each student).

For solving the question, regarding what types of learning dynamicity is better: interactive or adaptive, it is important to understand that we are living in a new world which faces the 4st industrial revolution rules in terms of metacognition, innovation, creativity, competence, experience, intuition and other transdisciplinary knowledge, skills and attitudes, so important for sustainable world. Therefore, for sustainable living it is important to design digital textbook on the base on new didactic model instead on using the instructional design model.

Global challenges impact on design digital textbooks interfaces is, first of all, about networking and new models of information, communication, cognition and assessment. The world is already hyperconnected. Everywhere is presented various forms of ubiquitous communication, in which learners are involuntary 'connected' through channels and networks in real—virtual learning environments, where they are more exalted to learn how to plan, model, create knowledge, establish connections then to hear bored lessons about old things and theories.

On the other hand, globalization in education refers to "cognitive shift, new relevancy spaces and new forms of subjectivities" (Macgilchrist and Christophe 2011, p. 155). This means that knowledge is not fixed, cut up in pieces and handed over, but rather (co)created by transacting with prior tacit knowledge, the curriculum, and other learners. It is a time to think about fundamental challengers regard a new educational ideal. There are some indicators: learning in/within local and/or global, real and/and virtual networks, where all resource and tools are available in order to offer students opportunity to learn anytime and anywhere.

For final decision regarding the interactivity or/and additivity in design of textbooks' interfaces let us analyses the applicability of a new educational ideal: "Professionalism, planetary thinking and cultural pluralism". Thus, the actual teachers and students are focused on a new strategy for learning the best methods and techniques in order to solve tasks in an professional competitive way. They are looking for innovative and creative solutions to protect the planet through 'absorbing' the global changes in culture, technology, ergonomics and ecology of learning and to propose adequate methodologies and educational technologies for sustainable education and development. The last, but not the least thing in interface design refers on cultural pluralism focusing on keeping cultural identity and autonomy of teacher and student.

5.5 Immersive Interfaces or/and Collaborative Assessment?

The 4th industrial revolution has accelerated the high technology acceptance on education. According to Passut (2016) with reference to Michio Kaku presentation at ISTE 2016, educators are going to have to stress concepts and principles, rather than the drudgery of memorization. The interface design for learning will take into account biotechnology, nanotechnology and artificial intelligence that will drive the economy in next future. For the driving of own live in a new economy, the actual students should be more creative, innovative, and intelligent.

Since now, psychological and behavioral actions of the actual students are shaping design for seeking a new intellect, energy, and emotion within various learner-centered learning environments. Such environments are immersive both for teacher(s) and for students. Thus, according to Dede (2009, p. 66), the immersion can enhance education by enabling multiple perspectives, situated learning and transfer. Typically, this is done by shifting between an exocentric and an egocentric frame of reference. Thus, the exocentric frame provides a view of an object, space, or phenomenon from the outside. Therefore, immersive learning is a form of learning in which teacher can control what experiences learners have, the feedback they receive, the opportunities they have to see both short-term and long-term consequences.

In designing for the immersive learning, it is combined actional, symbolic and sensory factors. According to Pagano (2013), the *immersive learning environment* is a framework of interactive learning environment, either physically or virtually. If this model is designed on the base of instructional systems design model, the learning scenarios are replicable. Does learning outcomes are replicable? The issue of replicability can be analysed on the base on concept "immersive digital learning tool". Such a tool, proposed by Pearson, aims to reimagine the textbook as a multimedia experience replete with videos, interactive exercises, and animated infographics. But, how to design such textbook in the most affordable way?

In concept of MetaSystems Learning Design, the most affordable model of design aim to increase the vitality of the generative structure of competence. Oddly enough, the ability to self-regulate own learning, as well as the most useful knowledge, skills and attitudes are not depend on what instructional approach or standards schools adopts. More important is with which (meta)cognitive thesaurus students come in life and how it was developed during lifelong learning. Therefore, digital learning can influence genotype and phenotype development in the positive or/and negative way, first, because use digital interfaces and learning environments.

Digital immersive interfaces allows students to develop own strategy for learning. If teachers accept other models instead of classical teaching, the students will only read, write or make calculus, but also, will develop own textbooks. In plus, there are multiple innovative ways to develop digital content for understanding, like *comics*. The importance of educational comics for design of textbooks is proved by Kim et al. (2016), Kußmann (2016), Sarada (2016), McGeown et al. (2016) and others.

The immersive interface design is not only about the principles and about norms of digital learning, but also about the possibility to develop new skills. One of such thing is using of hashtag. Thus, according to Echeveste (2014), the "hashtag" ("#") has become the go-to hot key for trending topics and Twitter discussions. They're prevalent on Twitter (where they got their start), but they have also seeped into Instagram, Google+, Vine, Tumblr, Pinterest, Facebook, Tagboard and even come up in Google searches and Google alert. For example, some of the hashtags may be used to find new digital textbooks.

References

Dede, C. (2009). Immersive interfaces for engagement and learning. *Science, 323*(5910), 66–69.

Browne, D., Totterdell, P., & Norman, M. (Ed.). (2016). *Adaptive user interfaces*. Elsevier.

Echeveste, S. (2014). 24 Examples of Using Hashtags for Teaching and Learning. http://www.emergingedtech.com/2014/11/ways-to-use-hashtags-for-teaching-and-learning/

ERC. (2016). Frontier research. https://erc.europa.eu/glossary/term/267

Frick, T. W. (1991). Restructuring Education through Technology. *Phi Delta Kappa Educational Foundation*. Bloomington: Indiana. https://www.indiana.edu/~tedfrick/fastback/fastback326.html

Gandhi, N. (2015). Industry 4.0—Fourth industrial revolution. http://scn.sap.com/community/manufacturing/blog/2015/06/30/industry-40–fourth-industrial-revolution

Guhlin, M. (2002). Methods That Work: Educator Competencies for Technology in Public Schools. http://files.eric.ed.gov/fulltext/ED466798.pdf

Kim, J., Chung, M. S., Jang, H. G., & Chung, B. S. (2016). The use of educational comics in learning anatomy among multiple student groups. *Anatomical Sciences Education*.

Kostolányová, K., & Šarmanová, J. (2016). Individualisation and personalisation of education-modern trend of eLearning. *International Journal of Continuing Engineering Education and Life Long Learning, 26*(1), 90–104.

Kußmann, J. (2016). Comics in the Bavarian Academic High School. *Novel Perspectives on German-Language Comics Studies: History, Pedagogy, Theory*, 67.

Lockee, B., Moore, D., & Burton, J. (2016). Foundations of programmed instruction. http://www.aect.org/edtech/20.pdf

Macgilchrist, F., & Christophe, B. (2011). Translating globalization theories into educational research: Thoughts on recent shifts in Holocaust education. *Discourse: Studies in the Cultural Politics of Education., 32*(1), 145–158.

McGeown, S. P., Osborne, C., Warhurst, A., Norgate, R., & Duncan, L. G. (2016). Understanding children's reading activities: Reading motivation, skill and child characteristics as predictors. *Journal of Research in Reading, 39*(1), 109–125.

Midoro, V. (2005). A Common European Framework for teachers' professional profile in ICT for education. Ortona, Italy. Edizony Menabo Didactica.

Network, F. L. (2014). The four pillars of FLIP™. http://www.flippedlearning.org/cms/lib07/VA01923112/Centricity/Domain/46/FLIP_handout_FNL_Web.pdf

Pagano, K. O. (2013). Immersive learning. Designing for authetic practice. USA: American Society for Training and Development.

Passut, J. (2016). ISTE 2016: Michio Kaku Says Education Needs a Revolution. http://www.edtechmagazine.com/k12/article/2016/06/iste-2016-michio-kaku-says-education-needs-revolution

Railean, E. (2008). Electronic textbooks in electronic portfolio: a new approach for the self-regulated learning. *Proceedings of 9th International Conference on Development and Application Systems DAS 2008* (pp. 138–141). Suceava: Stefan cel Mare University of Suceava.

Salmon, R., Priestley, R., Mitchell, D., Carter, A., & Dohaney, J. (2016). Science in Society spreads its wings: An online course suite and integrative MOOC approach. In *Charting Flexible Pathways in Open and Distance Education* (pp. 208–210). http://conference.deanz.org.nz/wp-content/uploads/2014/07/DEANZ16-Conference-proceedingsFINAL.pdf#page=208

Sarada, P. A. (2016). Comics as a powerful tool to enhance English language usage. *IUP Journal of English Studies, 11*(1), 60.

Schwab, K. (2016). The fourth industrial revolution. Geneva: World Economic Forum. http://cormolenaar.nl/wp-content/uploads/2016/04/The-fourth-industrial-revolution.pdf

Sedig, K., Klawe, M., & Westrom, M. (2001). Role of interface manipulation style and scaffolding on cognition and concept learning in learnware. *ACM Transactions on Computer-Human Interaction (TOCHI), 8*(1), 34–59.

Silver, K. (2007). What Puts the Design in Interaction Design. http://www.uxmatters.com/mt/archives/2007/07/what-puts-the-design-in-interaction-design.php

The Glossary of Educational Reform. (2015). Scaffolding. http://edglossary.org/scaffolding/

The On-Demand Economy. (2016). Powering the future of the on-demand economy. https://theondemandeconomy.org/

Weber, G., & Brusilovsky, P. (2016). ELM-ART–An interactive and intelligent web-based electronic textbook. *International Journal of Artificial Intelligence in Education, 26*(1), 72–81. http://gdac.uqam.ca/inf7470/Articles/EL-MART%20etc.pdf

Glossary

Adaptive textbook A system, a textbook or an educational software in which content is tailored to students' knowledge, skills, preferences, learning styles etc. through capturing the answer and presenting a personalized learning path for reading and re-reading

Apps Is a self-contained program or piece of software designed to fulfil a particular purpose; an application, especially as downloaded by a user to a mobile device

Artefact Is a something observed in a scientific investigation or experiment that is not naturally present but occurs as result of the preparative or investigative procedure

Blended learning Defines a mix of face-to-face methodology (e.g. lecture, drill-and-practice etc.), instructional technology (e.g. videotape, CD-ROM, web-based training, film) and web-based multimedia instruction (e.g. live virtual classroom, self-paced instruction, collaborative learning, streaming video, audio, and text) in order to create a harmonious effect of learning

Cloud computing Is a model for enabling ubiquitous, convenient, on-demand network access to a shared pool of configurable computing resources (e.g., networks, servers, storage, applications, and services) that can be rapidly provisioned and released with minimal management effort or service provider interaction (NST Definition)

Comics Is a medium used in education to express ideas by images often combined with text or other visual information and presented to students in the form of juxtaposed sequence of panels of images in order to indicate a dialogue, narration, or other information

Crystal A piece of a homogeneous solid substance having a natural geometrically regular form with symmetrically arranged plane faces

© Springer Nature Singapore Pte Ltd. 2017
E.A. Railean, *User Interface Design of Digital Textbooks*,
Lecture Notes in Educational Technology, DOI 10.1007/978-981-10-2456-6

Digital brain Is a term used to define a bran that can effectively process information through filtering irrelevant data, storing things for reference, writing down ideas and much more actions and activities, but not use binary logic or binary addressable memory, and it does not perform binary arithmetic, like a computer

Digital device Is a term used to define a physical unit of equipment (i.e. computer, tablet, smartphone and others), which may be used for learning

Digital learning environment Is a subset of a learning environment in which learning is has facilitated by technology

Digital library Is a special collection of documents in organized electronic form with a focused collection of digital objects, artefacts, patterns and meta-patterns, which is available on the Internet or on CD/DVD disks

Digital Revolution Is the global big change from mechanical and analogue electronic technology to digital electronics for mass production and widespread use of digital logic circuits and its derived technologies, including computers, Internet, digital textbooks etc.

Digital screen media Is the visual content specially designed and formatted to be delivered from digital screen such as LED, LCD, and projector screens either indoors or outdoors in corporate and public spaces

Distributed learning Is a model of instructional delivery the content that includes a mix of web instruction, streaming video conferencing, television, video, audio, face-to-face classroom time in all possible combinations of traditional and digital activities

Educational software Refers to a software that has be used for teaching, learning and assessment in order to maximise the power of the computer

Electronic paper or e-paper Is the 'paper' of computers, laptops and smartphones, which is made of flexible material, requiring ultra-low power consumption, cheap to manufacture, easy and convenient to read

Episodic memory A portion of long-term memory that includes the human's collection of past experience, single, collective or associated emotions, that occurred at a particular time and place

Formal learning Is a form of learning delivered by trained teachers within a school, academy, college, institute or university

Formative assessment Is a type of assessment concerned with how judgments about the quality of students response can be used to shape and improve the students' competence by short circuiting the randomness and inefficacy of trial-and-error learning

Gamification Defines the practical 'application of elements used in the development of video games, such as mechanics and dynamics in other contexts unrelated to games, to generate more enjoyable and positive attitudes from the students (de Santana et al. 2016, p. 911)

Genotype Is complete heritable generic identity or a genetic makeup of a specific organism, which produce different effects regarding different situations and, therefore, results in some of the physical characteristics or behavioural reactions of the human' body during learning

Global network Is a technology-based communication network, which spans the Earth

Global society Is a term used to describe the contemporary society, aroused as a result of the digital globalisation within flows of data and competence development, in which all people have a good deal in common with one another

Hashtag Is a type of label, symbol or metadata tag used to find messages within a specific theme or content more easily. For this, the hashtag character is placed in front of a world or unspaced phrase, either in the main text of a message or at the end

Immersion A subjective impression that one is participating in a comprehensive and realistic experience

Independent learning A form of learning when an individual is able to think, act and pursue their own studies autonomously, without the same levels of support you receive from a teacher

Informal learning Is a form of learning, which typically takes place naturally as part of some other activity

Interactive textbook A subset of a digital textbook in which students interact with content in reading, writing, exercising, playing simulations, educational games, direct virtual labs, animate art, get extra help and other activities

Intrinsic programing Or branching programing is a model of design electronic training devices without assumption about the nature of the learning process

Intuitive learning Form of learning based on own student or/and teacher intuition that allow discovering some possibilities and relationships

LCD screen Or Liquid Crystal Display, is a panel of liquid crystal molecules to take certain patters, which block light or allow it through. Color LCD displays have green, blue and red sub-pixels in each pixel. The teacher can control the intensity of light in order to display images in millions of colors

Learning algorithm Is a term used in programed learning to define a machine code able 'to sort problems' and provide relevant solutions

Learning analytics Is the measurement, collection, analysis and reporting of data about learners and their contexts, for purposes of understanding and optimizing learning and the environments in which it occurs. A related field is educational data mining

Learning object According to Hodgins (1994), is a collection of content items, practice items, and assessment items that are combined based on a single learning objective

LED screen Is a flat panel display, a small display, or a component of a larger display or screen, which uses an array of light-emitting diodes as pixels for a video display. LEDs can be quickly switched on or off, allows control of light and do not consume as much energy

Lifelong learner is a term Used to define a person that have the capacity to learn and actively learn throughout adult life in various learning environments across disciplines and subjects, and beyond traditional schooling and education

Literacy Is a term used to define a flexible and sustainable command of a set of capabilities in the use and production of traditional text and new communication technologies with spoken language, print and multimedia

Medium for teaching and learning A particular form, method or a system of communication (such as play, portfolio, digital textbook, ibook, ebook) that are used for teaching and learning. The best medium is considered adaptive and interactive, and the worst—video and podcasts

Monographic textbook A subset of an digital or digitalised academic monograph for reading the primary research and original scholar view, presented at length the synthesized patterns during research of a subject

Multimodal text Is a digital text that includes two or more of the following semiotics systems: linguistic, visual, audio, gestural and spatial. In a multimodal text, the effects of the semiotic systems combination represents a holistic whole

Nexus Is a series of smartphones and tablets manufactured by Google and its hardware partners, which run the native Android operating system

Non-formal learning Is a form of learning which includes instructional activities provided by non-trained educators and without a formal curriculum

On-demand economy Economic activity created by digital marketplaces that fulfil consumer demand via immediate access to and convenient provisioning of goods and services

Perceptual learning The process of learning improved skills of perception, ranging from simple sensory discriminations, cognitive processes to complex categorizations of spatial and temporal patterns relevant to real-world expertise

Phenotype Is the visible actual physical expression, or characteristics, or trait of each individual, which could be changed or modified during lifelong learning or some unique circumstances or environments in which the person life or/and study

Podcasts A digital audio file made available on the Internet for downloading to a computer or portable media player, typically available as a series, new instalments of which can be received by subscribers automatically

Productive learning Is an approach of learning focused on creating something new and innovative; it is based on insight and innovation

Reproductive learning Is an approach of learning reflecting in memorisation of the information needed for assessment and focusing on discrete element without integration

Responsive Text is a term used to define the possibility of digital technology to reside the text's container and to have the text reflow inside it through dynamic updating

Self-directed learning Is the process of learning in which learner takes the initiative to choice, e.g. to take one or more courses from a curriculum or to choose the pre-designed modules like a video tape, workbook, special reading, etc.

Semantic memory A portion of long-term memory that includes facts acquired over a lifetime and processes ideas and concepts that are not drawn from the personal experience (e.g. names of colors, the sounds of letters, the capital of countries etc.)

Summative assessment Is concerning with summing up or summarizing the status of a student and is geared toward reporting at the end of a course especially for purposes of certification

Web Is a collection of linked documents, graphics, and sounds accessed over the Internet